HEAR!
HEAR!

Lloyd Duhaime

HEAR! HEAR!

125 YEARS OF DEBATE IN CANADA'S HOUSE OF COMMONS

**Illustrations by
Graham Pilsworth**

First published in 1992 by
Stoddart Publishing Co. Limited
34 Lesmill Road
Toronto, Canada
M3B 2T6

Canadian Cataloguing in Publication Data

Duhaime, Lloyd, 1959–
    Hear! hear! : 125 years of debate in Canada's
House of Commons

Includes bibliographical references.
ISBN 0-7737-2644-6

1. Canada — Politics and government. 2. Canada.
Parliament — Publication of proceedings. I.
Pilsworth, Graham, 1944–   . II. Title.

FC500.D85 1992   971   C92-094962-2
F1033.D85 1992

Typesetting: Tony Gordon Ltd.
Printed and bound in the United States of America

*Stoddart Publishing gratefully acknowledges the
assistance of the Canada Council, Ontario Arts
Council, and Ontario Publishing Centre in the
development of writing and publishing in Canada.*

To
Glenda Pryce

CONTENTS

▶▶▶▶▶▶▶▶▶▶▶▶▶

Preface
▶▶▶▶▶▶▶▶▶▶

THIS BOOK HAS BEEN a labour of love. Rummaging through the pages of 440 volumes of Hansard has been a trip through the history of Canada. I hope that you the reader will share my experience of a voyage back in time, listening to the former leaders of Canada speak of the events that have shaped this country — an experience possible until now only by travelling through the pages of Hansard.

My simple criteria for selecting excerpts have been historical or parliamentary significance or humour. Most speeches have been shortened to accommodate a wealth of fascinating material. In no instances have I added words, save a few minor editorial changes to improve readability. For example, during the early years of Hansard (1867–1874), the debates were not reproduced verbatim (with some exceptions, such as most of John A. Macdonald's speeches). Rather, they were third-person narratives. I have changed these excerpts so they read as they were originally delivered. Occasional spellings have been modernized.

At times, Hansard fails to insert comments that have evidently been made. In three instances in this book, I have reconstructed an excerpt from other historical documents or from ensuing discussion in the House: most of August 13, 1873; parts of the King–Bennett exchange on June 8, 1928; and "An hon. member: Shut up and sit down!" on December 15, 1964.

The way I identify members in the excerpts is slightly at

variance with Hansard. Hansard does not note a minister's constituency but does indicate the portfolio. In *Hear! Hear!*, ministers, speakers and members are styled as follows. Ministers of the Crown: "Donald Fleming — Minister of Finance (Eglinton)"; Speakers of the House: "Mr. Speaker — George Black (Yukon)"; regular members: "Gilles Grégoire (Lapointe)." Throughout *Hear! Hear!* a member's riding may appear immediately after his or her name, in parentheses, within the commentary or the excerpts.

I would like to acknowledge the invaluable help of my wife, Glenda Pryce. Without her constant support and encouragement, this book might still just be another crazy idea of mine. I would also like to thank Donald G. Bastian and Jack Stoddart of Stoddart Publishing for accepting this manuscript, Shaun Oakey, who did such a magnificent job of editing the final manuscript, and Graham Pilsworth for his inimitable artwork, which so distinctively illustrates these pages. There is a long list of other people to thank, including the personnel of the libraries of the Treasury Board of Canada and of the Privy Council of Canada, who so graciously allowed me access to their complete Hansard and biographical collections; Michael Graham of the Library of Parliament, who provided me with Hansard editions for 1871 through 1874, which will not be available to the public for some time yet; an endless number of former members of Parliament and National Press Gallery journalists who so kindly answered my questions, including Stanley Knowles, Paul Martin, Sr., John Warren and Paul Akehurst. Thanks also to my sisters Liza, Rochelle and Christine, as well as to David Scott, Jim Creskey, Willard Holmes and Dennis Cooney for reviewing my earlier manuscripts. Last, but not least, a special thanks to Jim Creskey, Katie Molloy and Rosaleen Dickson of the *Hill Times* newspaper, who publish my weekly "Best of Hansard" column, which inspired this book.

LLOYD DUHAIME
Ottawa, July 1, 1992

HEAR!
HEAR!

Introduction

▶▶▶▶▶▶▶▶▶▶▶▶▶▶▶▶▶

FOR 125 YEARS, FEDERALLY ELECTED men and women from all parts of Canada have met in Ottawa, in the council chamber of Canada, known as the House of Commons. Virtually every issue that has shaped the destiny of Canada has been debated within the walls of that chamber. This book is an attempt to present the best excerpts and the most significant moments of 125 years of Hansard reports, the colloquial name for the published, verbatim *Debates of the House of Commons*. (The designation "Hansard" was carried over from England, where the reports of the debates of the British parliament were published by Thomas Hansard and his descendants from 1812 until 1888.)

On October 17, 1977, Canada became one of the first democracies in the world to televise its parliamentary proceedings. Most Canadians have since become familiar with the verbal exchanges so often replayed on the national news and extracted from a 45-minute segment of each day's work in the House of Commons, known as Question Period. But in the early years of Canada's Parliament, the proceedings rarely took on a sharp, one-on-one character. If questions were to be asked of the ministry, they were submitted in writing. Members of the House and of the press gallery would wait anxiously for political leaders to reveal their positions during speeches that frequently lasted several hours. Many of the rare sharp, one-on-one exchanges that did occur in the House before the advent of

▶ 1

Question Period, as we now know it, are reproduced in this book.

In 1867, the 18,000 residents of Ottawa were welcoming the first government of the Dominion of Canada. The small lumber town had none of the social amenities of the larger cities, such as a theatre or a professional music hall. Politics was the entertainment of the times.

When the new and magnificent Parliament Building on Wellington Street was officially opened in 1866, residents were thrilled with the prospect of evenings in the public gallery of the House of Commons and the Senate, where they could watch the top political figures of the country in action, men like Sir John A. Macdonald, George-Etienne Cartier, Charles Tupper, Alexander Mackenzie and Edward Blake.

Although Ottawa was far outpopulated by other cities of the Dominion, its choice came about not by quiet negotiation but by Imperial command. In 1858, Queen Victoria chose the town as the permanent site for local government of the Province of Canada. It lay on the border between Upper and Lower Canada and boasted a thriving economy and a rail link with the American Grand Trunk railway network.

Less than thirty years earlier, residents of Lower and Upper Canada (today Quebec and Ontario), had suffered armed uprisings. During the summer and fall of 1837, groups of disgruntled settlers in both colonies clashed with British forces, intent on forcing political change. Upper Canada rebels wanted an independent republic. In Lower Canada, the rebellion had no predesigned purpose but was rather a combination of opposition to the blatant anti-French patronage of the British governor's advisors and the restlessness of a growing body of unemployed men.

Although the British forces easily quelled the rebellions, it caused the Imperial government to rethink its British North American policies. The response was to merge the two colonies into one body of government, the Province of Canada, subject to the strict legislative supervision of England. But in both

Canadas, the forced union was met with mixed feelings. In Quebec, in particular, some aspects of the 1840 Act of Union were impossible to tolerate, such as the attempt to prevent the use of the French language in Parliament and in the administration of government.

The first seat of the Union government was in Kingston, and it was later moved to new buildings in Montreal. But when legislation was tabled before the Union Parliament proposing compensation to Lower Canada rebels of 1837, English Montrealers took to the streets. They hurled stones at the Governor General and burned the Parliament buildings.

Imperial authorities then implemented a rotating system of venues for the seat of the Union Parliament, to alternate every three years between Quebec and Toronto. When Queen Victoria chose Ottawa, it was as the proposed capital of the United Provinces.

In the Union Parliament, majority governments were short-lived. Compounding the French–English divisions were other powerful groups such as the Montreal English community, still the commercial brokers of the country. Upper Canada's political cast included John Baldwin, George Brown and a young Kingston lawyer, John Macdonald. Their Lower Canada counterparts were Louis-Hippolyte Lafontaine, George-Etienne Cartier and Etienne-Pascal Taché. The large Lower Canada English community was represented by prominent businessmen such as Alexander Galt and John Abbott.

In 1842, Lafontaine allied himself with Baldwin to produce the first durable government in the Union Parliament, beginning a system of two first ministers that would last until Confederation. Prominent leaders in both the Quebec and Ontario caucuses managed to keep the support of enough members to control a slight majority in the United Parliament. But by the 1860s, neither the Liberal-Conservative (later the Conservative party) nor the Reform (later the Liberal party) leaders were able to keep any makeshift government together. Any semblance of party discipline had become unpredictable at best. For example, from 1862 to 1864, there had been two elections and four governments. Legislative development stagnated.

Then, suddenly, on June 14, 1864, the leader of the Ontario Liberals in the United Parliament, George Brown, announced that he would be willing to join with Macdonald and Cartier to form a coalition government committed to constitutional change. Within weeks, the political leaders of Parliament of the United Provinces, John Macdonald, George-Etienne Cartier, George Brown and Etienne-Pascal Taché came to the conclusion that the future lay in greater political independence from Britain. The idea stuck.

A hastily organized series of meetings in Charlottetown and Quebec in 1864 brought political leaders representing New Brunswick and Nova Scotia into the fold. Newfoundland delegates enthusiastically attended the meetings, but the Confederation resolutions that the Quebec conference had produced met with defeat in their local legislature. In Prince Edward Island, an election resulted in the defeat of the pro-confederate premier. Even in New Brunswick and Nova Scotia, the Confederation proposal met with opposition, but in the end both provinces kept their names on the proposal that went forward to the final Confederation conference, held in London, England, in 1866.

The London conference, chaired by John A. Macdonald, produced a final consensus on the division of powers between proposed federal and provincial governments, a consensus that would form the basis for the agreement with the Imperial government and later become a British law known as the British North America Act. The 37 participants at these conferences became known as the Fathers of Confederation.

In fact, as Macdonald and the 15 other delegates to the London conference would soon discover, debate on the British North America Act bored British parliamentarians. As essential as it was to residents of the colony, the proposal reached the House of Lords at a time when they were preoccupied with the loss of Britain's dominion over the oceans, and they were facing a backlog of domestic legislative work. But at least the Canadian delegation would return to Canada successful. With only 10 of 400 members present in the British House, the BNA Act received third reading on March 8, 1867. Amongst suggestions including Acadia, Britannia, Cabotia, Canadia, Columbia, Laurentia, New Britain, Septentrionalia and Ursalia, the British House chose Canada as the name for the new nation.

On March 28, Queen Victoria gave the BNA bill royal assent. Two months later, she proclaimed that the law would come into effect on July 1, 1867. Canada had become master of her own domestic political destiny.

Upon royal assent of the BNA Act, Queen Victoria asked Sir

John A. Macdonald to form a provisional government until national elections could be held. The Governor General of Canada, Lord Monck, had informed Macdonald as early as March 21 that he would be charged with the formation of the first government as premier. Monck officially authorized Macdonald, in writing, "to undertake the duty of forming an administration for the Dominion of Canada" on May 24, 1867.

Canada's Scottish-born first minister continued the conciliatory spirit of Confederation and succeeded in luring a number of prominent Liberals to his first cabinet, appointed on July 1. Cabinet oaths were administered to Liberal-Conservatives Edward Kenny as receiver general; Alexander Campbell as postmaster general; Hector Langevin as secretary of state of Canada; Jean-Charles Chapais as minister of agriculture, and George-Etienne Cartier as minister of militia and defence. From the ranks of the Reform party and of the Liberal party, Macdonald added the former premier of New Brunswick, Samuel Tilley, as minister of customs; 45-year-old William McDougall became minister of public works; William Howland, elected in the first general election in York West and soon to be the lieutenant-governor of Ontario, was sworn in as minister of inland revenue; Senator Adam Fergusson Blair became the first president of the Privy Council (until his sudden death in December); Adams George Archibald, a Nova Scotian, was appointed secretary of state for the provinces; and Peter Mitchell was appointed minister of marine and fisheries. Macdonald named himself minister of justice and completed Canada's first cabinet with the addition of independent Alexander Galt, member for Sherbrooke, and Canada's first minister of finance. To accommodate the Reformers and Liberals, Macdonald was forced to omit prominent Conservatives such as Dr. Charles Tupper, the former premier of Nova Scotia, and Thomas D'Arcy McGee of Montreal, but they offered the prime minister added support in the first Parliament of Canada. Of the 13 members of Macdonald's first cabinet, 11 were Fathers of Confederation.

The first federal election of the Dominion was held between August 7 and September 20, 1867. As there was no national election law, residents of Ontario, Quebec, Nova Scotia and New Brunswick voted according to their respective provincial laws. When the writs were returned, 101 Conservatives were elected. The opposition mustered 80 members. More importantly, Liberal Leader George Brown had been defeated in the riding of Ontario South. His absence and Macdonald's success in bringing several of the Liberal party's most promising members of Parliament into his cabinet, devastated the front benches of the opposition.

1
A Nation's First Steps
▶▶▶▶▶▶▶▶▶▶▶▶▶▶▶▶▶▶▶▶▶▶▶▶▶▶▶▶▶▶▶▶▶▶▶

DAY ONE
▶▶▶▶▶▶

ON WEDNESDAY, NOVEMBER 6, 1867, Ottawa witnessed the opening of Parliament. Shops were closed for the day, and at the mayor's request, houses were decorated with flags and banners. Armed forces personnel followed a detailed program, marching at midday onto the small hill upon which stood the main Parliament Building. The entrance on Elgin Street, all the way to the tower of the main building, was quickly lined with troops. The public galleries of the Senate and Commons chambers were packed with dignitaries as the elected members filed into the House. One by one, they found their desk and took the oath of office.

And so it was that at approximately 3:30 p.m. that day, Sir John A. Macdonald, 52, rose in the House of Commons of the new Dominion of Canada. No fewer than four future prime ministers were in attendance. Behind him sat Charles Tupper, the Cumberland, Nova Scotia, doctor; John Abbott from the riding of Argenteuil in Quebec and former mayor of Montreal; and Orangeman Mackenzie Bowell, representing the riding of Hastings North in Ontario. Across the aisle Alexander Mackenzie, the member for Lambton, and 34-year-old Edward Blake, the member for West Durham, reigned over the depleted opposition benches. Mackenzie and Blake gazed over at Macdonald as the hum from members quickly subsided. It would be the first address in the House of Commons.

► **RIGHT HON. SIR JOHN A. MACDONALD** — Prime Minister and Minister of Justice (Kingston): The House has just been instructed by the representative of her Majesty to elect a Speaker. I move that the hon. James Cockburn, member for the West Riding of Northumberland, do take the chair. Mr. Cockburn had sat in the legislature of the Province of Canada during two parliaments having been thrice elected. During that period, he was invited to become a member of the government. In 1864, he entered the government of which I had the honour of being a member, taking the office of Solicitor-General for Upper Canada. All his colleagues could speak of the skill with which he managed all the affairs of his department.

JOSEPH DUFRESNE (Montcalm): I would like to express my dissatisfaction at the nomination of Mr. Cockburn. The gentleman cannot speak the French language. It is to be regretted that, at the inauguration of a new system, greater respect was not shown Lower Canada. This is a matter of national feeling. In the Constitution of the Dominion it was provided that all official documents should be printed in both official languages, and the principle which lay at the foundation of the provision should be carried out in the nomination of a Speaker.

GEORGE-ETIENNE CARTIER — Minister of Militia and Defence (Montreal East): Mr. Cockburn does not speak French but he understands it and in that respect he is in the same position as Speakers of the Canadian House under the former constitution — such as Mr. Sandfield Macdonald, Henry Smith and Mr. Waldbridge. ◄

Dufresne had made his point even though the Senate, on the same day, had elected a French-Canadian and former mayor of Quebec City, Joseph Cauchon, as its first speaker. Clearly, Macdonald would not be given any *passe-droits*. From page one of Hansard, there would be an opposition in the House of Commons. Still, the Kingston lawyer was in control of Parliament. His dominance was so complete that the 1872 directory of Parliament described members as either Liberal or "a supporter of Sir John Macdonald."

Yet the first sparks had jumped in Canada's new House of Commons. Cockburn was unanimously elected Speaker and conducted to the chair by Macdonald. A lawyer by profession, Cockburn had won his West Northumberland seat by acclamation and was an ardent supporter of Macdonald.

In accordance with British parliamentary tradition, adjournment followed, as it would not be proper for the House to entertain any further business until the Crown had tabled its intentions for the session in the first speech from the throne.

While the country had the benefit of more than a hundred years of British democratic experience, the combination of a new Dominion and an aggressive and unpolished constituency would lead to a lifetime of challenges for Macdonald. The new prime minister had before him a House that needed rules of order, members of Parliament who needed salaries, and a country that did not unanimously support confederation.

By choice, he remained very much in the background during the first months of the new Parliament. The throne speech had promised much, and the legislative terrain was begging for action. Territory to the west needed settlers, and the east needed reassurance that confederation with British North America was in their best interest. There were laws to write, provincial government concerns to deal with, as well as treaties to negotiate with native Canadians. Coins had to be minted, a police force organized and somehow an interprovincial railway had to take track.

"THAT PESTILENT FELLOW HOWE!"
▶▶▶▶▶▶▶▶▶▶▶▶▶▶▶▶▶▶▶▶▶▶

PROVINCIAL ELECTIONS held in Nova Scotia in September of 1867 swept the pro-confederates out of office. Anti-confederates won not only 36 of 38 seats in the provincial assembly but also 18 of 19 Nova Scotia ridings in the 1867 federal election. In October of 1867, Prime Minister Macdonald wrote to a friend and boasted, "Our majority is too large. Nova Scotia, on the other hand, has declared, so far as she can, against confederation. But she will be powerless for harm, although that pestilent fellow, Howe, may endeavour to give us some trouble in England."

When the First Session of the First Parliament began, Macdonald's biggest fear was that the anti-confederates from Nova Scotia would not even attend the proceedings of the House. But appear they did. On Friday, November 8, 1867, their leader, Joseph Howe, rose to respond to the speech from the throne and explain the objections of Nova Scotia to confederation.

► **JOSEPH HOWE** (Hants): Mr. Speaker, the people of my province feel they have been legislated out of the Empire by being legislated into this Dominion. They will read His Excellency's speech with sorrow and humiliation, and not gratification. The bill was passed in the face of a petition of 31,000 of the people of Nova Scotia. They did not ask to throw out the bill, merely to delay it until the Nova Scotians had time to pronounce upon it at the hustings. There is, therefore, on the part of Nova Scotia, certainly no room for congratulation for the manner in which it has been treated by the Mother Country. Then this new nation, as it is called, we are told, is soon to be extended from the Atlantic to the Pacific. It has no army to defend it, no navy to protect its shipping. It has been one of the great objections of Nova Scotians to this Dominion scheme that the minister of militia might march their young men out of their country to defend a corner of the earth hundreds of miles away from them.

I do not believe that the people of Nova Scotia will ever be satisfied to submit to an act which has been forced upon them by such unjust and unjustifiable means. What is the union but a mere act of Parliament? If bad, its repeal may be agitated for. Yet this union act has been spoken of as something against which it is treason to say a word. The people of my province were tricked into this scheme. ◄

For thirteen months, Howe would carry the banner for the anti-confederate Nova Scotians. Though it would prove to be a losing cause, the position of Howe and his colleagues in the House, for the brief time that their opposition lasted, gave the first Parliament a three-party character which, once lost, it would not again experience for 54 years.

INVITATION TO NEWFOUNDLAND
►►►►►►►►►►►►►►►►►►►►►►►►

O N MAY 24, 1869, delegates from the Island of Newfoundland arrived in Ottawa to negotiate terms for accession into the Canadian confederacy. On June 3, Finance Minister John Rose stood triumphantly in the House and announced that the government would be tabling resolutions "on the subject of Newfoundland" at a very early date. Government members broke into cheers.

Five days later, Rose himself led off the debate and moved that Newfoundland be invited to join Canada. He pointed to 1,557 vessels owned by Newfoundlanders; that 10,000 seamen were employed in the fisheries; and that "Newfoundland was wholly a consuming population, raising nothing and manufacturing nothing."

Opposition members expressed their annoyance with the tardiness of the measure, tabled so late in the session. The member for Westmoreland, New Brunswick, Albert Smith, added: "Why, it appears that one-fifth of the entire revenue of the Island has to be devoted to the support of the poor."

Joseph Howe had only recently abandoned his anti-confederate stance. Prime Minister Macdonald had even managed to lure the member for Hants into the cabinet, giving him the prestigious position of president of the Privy Council. Howe had earlier explained to the House that faced with failure in his numerous petitions to the British government to allow Nova Scotia out of the Canadian confederation, he had decided to try to negotiate with Macdonald for better terms for his province. To his surprise, Macdonald was a sympathetic listener and offered improved federal subsidies. On January 30, 1869, Macdonald announced "better terms" for Nova Scotia and the acceptance of a cabinet position by Howe.

It was Howe, in one of his first speeches as a minister, who provided the most interesting commentary on the proposal that Newfoundland become a province of Canada.

► JOSEPH HOWE — President of the Privy Council (Hants): Sir, no doubt that Canada, for her own purposes, has formed this confederacy.

She has taken step after step with a view to consolidation. In that view, the acquisition of Newfoundland is a matter of prime importance. Newfoundland is to us a necessity. We may throw off the great west but we cannot throw off Newfoundland. It lies in the very chops of the channel, as it were, at the very entrance of our new Dominion. Newfoundland is worth having for her own value and importance. Her higher political importance, in looking at the future, can not be over-rated.

The five North American Colonies had all their trials and tribulations in the past, but Newfoundland has had more than her share. She is the oldest colony on the continent, discovered first and occupied first. From two or three summers which I spent in that colony, what I then saw made me more willing to admit this people into the confederacy. In their towns I found as educated, refined and wealthy a people as any on the mainland. In point of beauty and social attractiveness, the women of Newfoundland are magnificent, many of them being equal to two-thirds of a man!

The political celebrities of Newfoundland are men of enlarged mind and true political sagacity, never wanting to fight battles where difficulties arise. I hope to see some of these men in the service of the confederacy.

The seal-fishery is a rich one, peculiarly their own and can not be taken from them. In a small town in which I was one day, I met a fine sturdy fisherman with a gin bottle about as big as a clothes basket, who had got in $10,000 worth of seals in four weeks! ◄

After Howe, the House heard from the Liberal opposition member Edward Blake. Blake was quick to agree with the principle of the resolution, but on June 10 he moved "that Newfoundland should retain its public lands." Macdonald rose next and stated categorically that the proposed amendment would defeat the whole scheme. Blake's amendment was put to a vote and lost on a 48–94 division. Before the day was over, Rose's resolution was approved by the House of Commons.

But to no avail. Armed with the Canadian offer for unification, Prime Minister Frederick Carter of Newfoundland called an election for November 1869. The Confederation battle raged throughout the island. Anti-confederate propaganda read: "Let us keep our fisheries to ourselves! Never give to Canada the right of taxing us! Let us never change the Union Jack for the Canadian beaver!" Carter tried to use the United States as an example of the prosperity union could bring. When the election results were in, union with Canada was soundly defeated as 21 anti-confederates were elected to the 30-member Newfoundland Parliament.

UPRISING IN THE NORTHWEST
▶▶▶▶▶▶▶▶▶▶▶▶▶▶▶▶▶▶▶▶

IN THE EARLY DAYS of French fur traders and their excursions west of the Great Lakes, interracial relationships were encouraged. For the French *coureurs de bois*, female companionship was possible only with native women. The granting of Rupert's Land (which included modern-day northern Quebec, northern Ontario, all of Manitoba and most of Saskatchewan — a territory five times the size of France) to the Hudson's Bay Company in 1670, and the establishment of numerous trading posts by its employees, added to the numbers of "half-breeds," or persons of Native and European descent, known as the Métis. By 1869, the Métis had established permanent communities and were dominant in Rupert's Land.

The leader of the 1870 insurrection was Louis Riel. Riel was relocated from his St.-Boniface Métis homestead at an early age; his education was sponsored by a wealthy Montreal family. Some years later, he began an apprenticeship to the profession of law but quickly became disillusioned with the favouritism and pressures of an urban commercial environment. The final straw came when he was prevented from marrying his Montreal sweetheart because he was part Native.

Riel abandoned Montreal on the very day that the British North America Act became law, on July 1, 1867. A year later, he was back in St.-Boniface and found his people primed for conflict. American intelligence agents were stirring up the population of the territory towards annexation with the United States. Several greedy Hudson's Bay Company employees were doing their utmost to consolidate their personal land holdings before the anticipated union with Canada. For the Métis, droughts and grasshopper plagues had devastated their modest harvests in 1867 and again in 1868. Their other food source, the buffalo, were long gone from the banks of the Red River. Rupert's Land was ripe for turmoil.

At about the same time, east of Lake Superior, Cartier's long-heralded Canadian Pacific Railway was slowly stalking deeper into northern Ontario, closing in on Métis territory. Rail workers were, for the most part, Anglo-Protestants and patriotic to the core. As the railway workers inched towards the northwestern border of Ontario, laden with ill-concealed prejudice towards Native people, they overran the farmland and communities of the Métis with the arrogance of medieval lords. Stories of their behaviour quickly travelled west.

The Queen's Proclamation of the Northwest Territories Act, which would finalize the transfer of the territory to the Canadian government, was scheduled for December 1, 1869. In the fall of 1869, Macdonald shuffled his cabinet and appointed Joseph Howe as secretary of the provinces. Howe travelled to the Red River and met with local residents, who included the Métis and a small group of European settlers. His stay in the territory would be the subject of much discussion in the House when the session resumed in March.

The first line drawn in the Red River Rebellion occurred when a group of Métis intercepted a team of Canadian surveyors at the Red River. Days later, the newly appointed lieutenant-governor of the territory, William McDougall, and his large stately crew (which included cooks and servants) was stopped at the American border and denied entry to the territory. A summit of Métis men was hastily called in Fort Garry and a "national committee" was organized. In response, Red River residents loyal to Canada organized an armed resistance to the Métis proclamation, and although the Métis were able to secure their surrender, this set the stage for what would become a violent encounter.

A number of the resistance fighters escaped Riel's guard and attempted once again to raise the people against the Fort Garry committee. They were easily rounded up and again jailed in Fort Garry. Amongst them was a surveyor by the name of Tom

Scott. Scott, an arrogant Protestant, would not cease taunting his captors or keep quiet in his cell. An impromptu Métis military court was quickly constituted and within twenty-four hours, Scott was court-martialled on charges of taking up arms against the provisional Métis government, sentenced to death and executed by firing squad. It was March 4, 1870.

News was slow to travel in 1870. Although they had been laid under the Atlantic Ocean, telegraph lines did not yet span into the northwest. On March 14, the minister of militia and defence, Sir George-Etienne Cartier, informed the House that, contrary to rumour, "the Government has received no information that there has been any blood shed or loss of life."

It was but a brief calm before the full fury of the violent actions of the Red River Métis hit the nation's capital. On March 26, the Toronto *Globe* published a sensational eye-witness account of the murder of Thomas Scott. Ontario's Protestant population was furious that one of their own would be so contemptuously executed by what they perceived as lawless renegades running amok in a Canadian territory. Armed with the *Globe* story, Edward Blake insisted, on March 29, that Macdonald give an explanation to the House.

"The government has received no official or reliable information of a man being shot at Fort Garry, by order of a provisional government," stated Prime Minister Macdonald. "I have received a private telegram from a gentleman at St. Paul's, informing me that a person named Scott had been shot by a provisional government."

Once apprised of the uprising, Macdonald secretly ordered payment to the Hudson's Bay Company delayed so that the territory would remain under the legal authority of the company and of England. His strategy was simple enough: subdue the uprising with patience, understanding and kindness.

But within days, it was obvious that the young and fragile, bilingual and bicultural fabric of Canada was to face its first real challenge. Macdonald and Cartier had grossly misjudged the fears and pride of the Métis. Back at Fort Garry, Riel and his gang had passed the point of no return.

Macdonald did not want to share the day-to-day reports with

his colleagues in the House, for this would have meant daily questioning and criticism of government actions, which, as the land was still under British authority, required telegraphic coordination with Imperial authorities in London, England. In the House, he eventually confirmed the court-martial execution and added: "The two governments are acting in accord and unison and with the one object in view, that of retaining that country as a portion of Her Majesty's Dominions, and of restoring law and order therein. The line of conduct has been settled upon. What that line of conduct may be, must be for the present withheld from the House and I am quite sure the House will not ask nor expect me to say more." That was wishful thinking. Mackenzie immediately insisted that troops be sent by ship across Lake Superior to Thunder Bay, and from there to Fort Garry.

As the prime minister had intimated, the government's response was being developed behind the scenes but was not yet complete. Two weeks passed. Soon, members began to ask for the final report of the special commissioner Macdonald had accredited. Macdonald stated that Donald Smith's report had still not been handed to him. Opposition members picked up information as they could, mostly from daily newspapers. Finally, Joseph Dufresne (Montcalm), concerned for the safety of the three delegates sent to Ottawa by the provisional government of the Northwest, confronted the prime minister in the House.

"They were arrested as parties to a certain crime committed in the Northwest," declared Dufresne, referring to the court-martial execution of Scott. "They are going to be imprisoned tomorrow. Some few days ago, they were threatened by a mob of being lynched. I hope that the government will tell us in what manner they looked upon these delegates."

All the prime minister would say was that no delegate had yet officially come before the government, although he knew that three members of Riel's provisional government were in town and were being harassed by local officials. But Macdonald wanted a peaceful settlement, and as early as April 25, he met privately with the three provisional government delegates,

Judge John Black, Father Noel Joseph Ritchot and Alfred Scott. To get an acceptable resolution to the crisis, he had to stay low and deal privately; not in the House of Commons. Not all members of the House agreed, and certainly not the members of the opposition.

As the end of the session loomed, expected in a few weeks, the limits of opposition members' patience began to wane. Again the next day, Mackenzie, sounding like a broken record, asked, "Are the reports of the Northwest Commissioners to be distributed today?" Macdonald answered, "Tonight or tomorrow."

By Friday, April 29, the House was ready to explode. Macdonald had been seen drinking the night before. Then, as the House prepared itself for the day's sitting, Macdonald was seen wandering the halls, intoxicated. As Cartier was frantically putting together the final touches on a deal with the Northwest delegates that would form the basis for a bill for Parliament, cabinet ministers Joseph Howe and Sir Francis Hincks (North Renfrew) were sent to the front.

"I would like to ask the government when the bill in relation to the Northwest, which has been promised for the last two or three days, is likely to be submitted to the House," began McDougall.

"Not today," replied Howe. "I am afraid not until Monday. I would much prefer that one or other of the leaders of the House were present to answer this question."

Then, Luc-Hyacinthe Masson (Soulanges) suggested that the House adjourn for a fortnight or a month "to give good time to well consider the matter." He was shouted down. The House did eventually adjourn for the weekend, but without further progress on either the situation at Red River or the much-anticipated Manitoba bill.

On Monday, May 2, well aware that the House had by then but little time left to debate the bill, the prime minister walked into the House carrying a large scroll. Having spent the weekend recovering from his drinking binge, he walked over to the clerk's table and dramatically unrolled a map of a proposed province of Manitoba.

► **RIGHT HON. SIR JOHN A. MACDONALD** — Prime Minister and Minister of Justice (Kingston): I rise, Sir, with the consent of the House, to submit the result of our deliberations for the framing of a constitution for the country heretofore known as Rupert's Land and the Northwest territory.

The name of the province was a matter of taste and should be considered with reference to euphony and with reference as much as possible to the remembrance of the original inhabitants of that vast country. Fortunately the Indian languages for that section of the country give us a choice of euphonious names and it is considered proper that the province which is to be organized, shall be called Manitoba. I suppose there will be no objection to the name which is an old Indian name, meaning "The God who speaks — the speaking God."

It is necessary, also, that the fears of an Indian war and foreign aggression, which have been raised, very naturally, in the minds of the people of that country, from recent unhappy events, should be allayed. For all these reasons it is fitting and proper that a force should be there to cause law and order to be respected. An arrangement has been made between Her Majesty's government and the government of Canada for the despatch of an expedition. That expedition will be a mixed one, comprised partly of Her Majesty's regular troops, and partly of Canadian militia, and from all those whom we have had an opportunity of seeing from the Northwest, we are told that a force sent in that spirit, and commanded by an officer of Her Majesty's service, under Her Majesty's sanction, will be received not only with kindness, but with gladness. The force will be comprised of about one-fourth of Her Majesty's regular troops, and three-fourths Canadian Militia, and the expenditure will be borne in the same proportion. This militia was called upon to volunteer from different districts, and such has been the alacrity displayed, that if a force was proposed to assume the proportion of an army there would be no trouble in getting the men. Happily that necessity does not, I am fain to believe, exist. ◄

Compared to its modern-day dimensions, the proposed province was tiny and included only territory south of Lake Winnipeg and fifty miles on each side of the Red River. Opposition Leader Mackenzie was caught off guard, having received no advance copy of the final legislative package. "Sir, it is manifestly impossible to discuss the bill at this time," he began. "But it does seem a little ludicrous to establish a little municipality in the Northwest of 10,000 square miles — about the size of two or three counties in Ontario — with a population of 15,000 people, having two chambers, and a right to send two members to the Senate and four to the House here. The whole thing has such a ludicrous look that it only puts in one's mind some of the incidents in *Gulliver's Travels!*"

The leader of the opposition also criticized the land reserve policy, which provided for special scrips of land for Métis settlers and a large Indian reserve. Macdonald jumped on the subject and informed the House that "the expectation is that there will be a large influx of emigrants from Europe or from Canada. There is a fear that emigrants from the American States, accustomed to dealing with the Indians as enemies, would shoot them down and cause great disturbances. The necessity arose to have a small but active force of cavalry to act as mounted police, so that they could move rapidly along the frontier to repress disturbances. It was not proposed to make the force more than 200 men. They will be drilled as mounted riflemen and be disciplined as a military body, but act as constabulary." His reply lay the foundation of the Royal Canadian Mounted Police.

The prime minister's large majority in the House held him through the long and tenuous debate. He had hoped that his Manitoba bill would sail through without too much dissent. In fact, when Liberal opposition members noted the omission of Portage la Prairie, a large English settlement 60 miles west of Fort Garry along the Assiniboine River, Macdonald allowed the amendment to his bill. Anything to secure second reading.

Opposition leader Mackenzie also felt the pressures of time. Adjournment loomed only nine days away, and the patience of the official opposition had run its course. On the next day, immediately after the call to order of the House of Commons, he jumped to his feet. "Sir, days and weeks have been totally lost in consequence of the utter want of preparation for the business of the country." William McDougall added that no delegates "appointed by Riel and his gang" should be received.

► **MR. MACDONALD:** If the hon. gentleman wishes to lose that country he will pursue this course.

WILLIAM MCDOUGALL (North Lanark): We shall not lose it if you do your duty!

MR. MACDONALD: I do mine as well as you did yours where you were! The delegates are representatives of the people, elected by a Council of the inhabitants. Until those gentlemen came to Ottawa, and until the government of Canada heard in what way the government of Canada was distasteful to them, it was out of the question to prepare a bill for the government of the territory. Can a Constitution be prepared in a day or two?

MR. MACKENZIE: Sir, the hon. gentleman told us that he would not receive the delegates.

MR. MACDONALD: No! No! Directly the reverse!

MR. MACKENZIE: He said so to others and personally to myself. I am positively sure he said so. He has said today that they were the delegates of the people. But I give to that assertion an emphatic: "no!" This meeting, or Council was held in the Court house. Riel had a large armed force under his direct control. Armed guards surrounded the building in which the meeting was held and guards held the gate of the stockade. A reign of terror existed. With this armed force, Riel threatened daily the delegates, both French and English, who attempted to express any opposition to his demands or vote contrary to his wishes. I am not willing that they should be recognized as the representatives of the people. What is the loyalty of the premier? I will not sit in this House without raising my indignant protest against the reception of those men nominated by Riel as delegates.

MR. MACDONALD: Sir, the government is endeavouring to restore peace and order and we would do right if they were not subject to these attacks. ◄

Hansard states that "the subject then dropped." There was no time to waste in completing the legislative task at hand. Macdonald led his government into the second reading debate, which began on May 4, of the bill to establish the government of the province of Manitoba. It was the same document as the bill presented on first reading except that the proposed boundary had been extended to include Portage la Prairie. Just after midnight, Prime Minister Macdonald moved and secured second reading. The bill was referred to the committee of the whole, to be debated again (chaired by a deputy speaker, the committee of the whole includes all members of the Commons, and meets in the House immediately after second reading for a detailed, clause-by-clause study of a bill). Quickly, Macdonald kept up his momentum. "I move the House sit on Saturday and that the government measures take precedence." The motion carried. It was 1 a.m.

The next day, just as Macdonald was preparing for lunch in his office, and another long day in the House, he suffered a terrible seizure. Rumours rushed through Parliament. From May 6 onwards, Cartier would lead the government as his prime minister passed gallstones amidst life-threatening pain. Tactfully, Mackenzie asked Cartier what was to happen to the Manitoba bill.

"The reason why the government has not gone on with the Manitoba bill was the sudden illness of the minister of justice, who has been seized, I regret to say, with spasms as he was preparing to come down to the House," offered Cartier. "We are desirous that this measure, which was one in which the minister of justice took great interest, should be held over. John A. Macdonald would like to be in his seat when the measure goes through Parliament."

"Mr. Speaker," responded Mackenzie, "I can only express my regret at the illness of the premier, and say that so far as I am personally concerned, I would not insist on taking up the measure during the absence of the minister of justice."

Another recess for the government. Again, but this time for practical reasons rather than political ones, the House of Commons would lose an opportunity to consider the conditions under which this small western territory was to join the Canadian confederation. Just before the House adjourned on May 6, Cartier again reported on Macdonald's health. The danger of Macdonald's condition had not yet been ascertained. The stature of Macdonald, however, within Canadian political society was evident in the spontaneous accommodation of all members with regards to his Manitoba bill.

"Has the hon. gentleman no authentic information as to the real condition of the premier?" asked the Liberal member for Chateauguay, Luther Holton. "We would like to know, as there is a good deal of anxiety felt as to his condition."

"He is not well enough to be taken from his office to his house," replied the minister of militia and defence, George-Etienne Cartier, "but is lying there asleep."

The Manitoba bill, Louis Riel, Thomas Scott . . . nothing seemed to matter so much anymore. Reports of Macdonald's imminent death raced along the telegraph wires. Cartier rose in the House on May 7. He quickly requested and carried a motion "that government orders have precedence every day during the remainder of the session." This, by forcing opposition motions to the bottom of the order paper, would pre-empt any opposition stalling tactics. Then came official news on Macdonald's condition.

► **JAMES BROWN** (Hastings West): Sir, yesterday I called to see Sir John A. Macdonald, but found Dr. Grant in attendance and returned to my house, but an hour after I received a note to go back and found Sir John A. Macdonald pulseless and in a state of collapse. The remedies applied by Dr. Grant are so far effectual as to relieve him. The disease, I believe, is biliary calculus, from which he suffered excruciating agony till nine at night. He has spent a very restless night, and at nine this morning there was a slight improvement, which was confirmed since then. But he was still unable to be removed and, of course, to attend in the House. ◄

The clock struck midnight and cut debate short on Saturday, May 8, but not before another division on the bill, this time in committee of the whole, which again favoured the government.

It was 3:25 p.m. when the House reconvened on May 9, 1870. "Sir John A. Macdonald is doing much better," announced Cartier. And save a few sputters of life from the most desperate of the Grits, the opposition had been painfully beaten by Saturday's divisions. Finally, it seemed, the debate would centre on the articles of the bill and not on Louis Riel, Thomas

Scott or Joseph Howe — at least, not for a few brief moments. The fight was not over yet.

► **MR. MCDOUGALL:** Mr. Speaker, it seems to some persons that the acts of Riel are nothing. One hon. member has said, with lugubrious countenance, if they were noticed there would follow a war of race against race. Did he mean to say that there are any persons in Canada who sympathized with the rebels? The insurrectionary party is the most disreputable inhabitants of the country, and were collected together by a bar-room loafer.

MR. HOWE: The time, I believe, has arrived when the House must feel that some explanations on my part are called for. The hon. member never loses an opportunity of saying a savage and offensive thing in an exceedingly disagreeable and unpleasant manner. Not only did the hon. member assail me, but some of his followers — all the small curs, "Tray, Blanche, and Sweetheart!" One after the other ran barking at my heels. I felt a little like the man who was stuck in the pillory for an hour, and after everybody had pelted dead cats and brick-bats at him for their own amusement, exclaimed at the end of the hour, "my turn has come," and then got up and returned all the dead cats and brick-bats at the heads of his tormentors!

When I came up from my own province and joined this government, I accepted the policy of Confederation. I had known the Hon. Mr. McDougall — I beg his pardon for naming him — for some years. From the moment I sat down with him in the Privy Council this was his position: Mr. Fergusson Blair was dead, Mr. Howland had been appointed Lieutenant-Governor of Ontario, and he sat there as the only Liberal, except my hon. friend from New Brunswick, Mr. Tilley, in the cabinet.

Now, if I have been anything all my life in politics, I have been a Liberal. The party with which I acted in Nova Scotia, and which for many years I had the honour of leading — was the Liberal party. We called ourselves Liberals and were not ashamed of the name. When I came up here, then, I found the hon. gentleman the only Liberal representing Canada in the government. He had my sympathy and, as far as I know, or can remember, an unkind word never passed between us. When I became Secretary of State for the Provinces, the proposition made to me to accept that office was made on his own sofa in his own house, with no one present but the premier, the hon. gentleman and myself.

What was the next step? I felt that I could not assume the duties of that office with justice to my own character, to this House, and with satisfaction to the country, without using every means in my power of acquiring that information with regard to the Northwest which it is now apparent not a man at the Council-board was possessed of. I consulted with that hon. member. He and I went up together to Thunder Bay to overlook the progress of the road-makers and to examine the approaches to the country. The first mistake he made was this: when we were at Thunder Bay, he should not have come back to Canada. If he had taken a canoe and gone quietly into the Northwest territory, he would have done an act of superlative wisdom for which he would have got infinite credit at this House. He preferred, however, to go into the territory in great state. He talks of my not stopping on the prairie to confer with him, but if any one could have seen the great cavalcade of carriages, the number of women and children in this train on that frosty morning, it would not have been wondered at that I did not stop. Why, Sir George Simpson, who for years was governor of the Hudson's Bay Company, or governor McTavish never went in such state through the country! Sir George Simpson in his frequent and arduous journeying over the country often went in a bark canoe attended by a few Indian guides and living upon the roughest fare. But the hon. gentleman went out there as a great satrap paying a visit to his province, with an amount of following, a grandeur of equipage and a display of pomp that was enough to tempt the cupidity of all the half-breeds in the country! That, I say, was his first blunder, and a great blunder it was!

The member for Lambton says I ought to have held meetings and "seen everybody" in the territory, explaining to them the intentions of this Dominion. But hon. members must see that in Winnipeg it is altogether a different matter. The population there were those French half-breeds who have since prevented the hon. gentleman's entrance into the territory. Now, I appeal to hon. gentlemen to say how it was possible for me to address them intelligibly, however anxious I might have been, when in early life I neglected to do what I advise every young man in Canada to do — to speak the French language fluently? Could I have addressed them in their own language with which alone they are familiar? Suppose I have called meetings and made speeches which would have had the effect of agitating the people there — one party siding with me and my views and another perhaps opposing them. ◄

Thus began the final hours of debate on the Manitoba bill, marked as it had started by a bitter personal exchange between the member for Hants and the member for North Lanark. More last-minute amendments and resolutions were put to the House by opposition members, demanding that special lands grants the bill proposed to give to the Métis, or "half-breeds," be repealed. Another called for a territorial government rather than full provincial status. During the final hours, well into the early hours of May 10, nine opposition motions were presented and fell. The House adjourned at 3:05 a.m. The next day, Cartier moved third reading. The bill had survived its fast-track through the House with a sole amendment: that of extending the borders of the proposed province of Manitoba to include Portage la Prairie. Just before third reading, Mackenzie stood and informed the House that it was useless to oppose the bill any longer. "The government declined, from first to last, to accept any amendment." But Mackenzie added that because of the urgency of having some form of government there, "so far as he was concerned, it might pass without any opposition whatever."

There remained but one more item of concern to members. Just before adjournment at midnight, May 11, Cartier announced that Parliament would be prorogued the next day at 3:30 p.m. As for the condition of the prime minister, the news was short but good.

► **MR. CARTIER:** I have at this moment received a bulletin from the medical gentleman who attends Sir John A. Macdonald, which I will read to the House, and I know these few lines will be heard and accepted with the greatest delight. It is:

> *I am happy to inform you that Sir John A. Macdonald is now, for the first time since his attack, resting on his right side. Truly yours,*
> *James Grant* ◄

Military expedition included, the Macdonald-Cartier Manitoba package had passed its final phase in the House. On Thursday, May 12, 1870, in the Senate, Governor General Lord Lisgar prorogued Parliament, ending the Third Session of this First Parliament of the Canadian Confederation, announcing royal assent to An Act to Amend and Continue the Act 32 and 33 Victoria, chapter 3, and to Establish and Provide for the Government of the Province of Manitoba. Parliament would not sit again until the following February.

Only a few doors away, the prime minister lay in his office. His condition prevented any movement. By the end of May, many expected that he would not survive. On June 2, he was moved to more comfortable quarters, the Speaker's chambers. From there on, his condition gradually began to improve. On July 2, he left Ottawa by steamship for two months of convalescence in Charlottetown.

Meanwhile, the military expedition had reached the Red River without incident. Riel had fled. Soon, other issues headed the federal cabinet agenda, and one in particular would command Macdonald's undivided attention. On February 27, 1871, Macdonald set out from Ottawa to join a joint commission of the United States and British governments to resolve outstanding disputes between the governments of those two countries. As Canadian external affairs were still managed by the Imperial government, the mandate of the commission included Canada–United States issues. The Canadian prime minister was gone from the capital for more than two months, leaving Cartier to introduce legislation to admit yet another province into Canada.

2

Growing Pains
▶▶▶▶▶▶▶▶▶▶▶▶▶▶▶▶▶▶▶▶▶▶▶▶

BRITISH COLUMBIA FOR $100-MILLION
▶▶▶▶▶▶▶▶▶▶▶▶▶▶▶▶▶▶▶▶▶▶▶▶▶▶

THE **ADMISSION** OF THE COLONY of British Columbia seemed to be only a matter of time. Canada, Great Britain and the colony itself all favoured the project. On May 10, 1870, three British Columbia unionist representatives left Victoria for San Francisco, where they boarded the American transcontinental railway, opened only the year before. After a 24-day journey, Robert Carral, Joseph Trutch and John Helmcken arrived in Ottawa and delivered a series of demands to the Canadian government.

The Pacific coast colony had a history similar to Canada's: initial possession and administration by the Hudson's Bay Company; military and border controversies with the United States; and British appropriation, political supervision and organization. The colony had also undergone its own measure of confederation in 1866 when the Imperial government merged the mainland and Vancouver Island into the United Colony of British Columbia.

But in other ways, British Columbia was distinct. Its population felt little natural affinity with Canada; British and American leanings were much stronger. A sudden gold rush in 1858 had contributed 30,000 to the population and settlements popped up along every river. But spurred on by an Imperial government increasingly concerned with the colony's growing public works debt, the population began to warm to the idea of confederation with Canada.

The delegation proposed the colony's terms to George-Etienne Cartier, the minister of militia and defence and deputy prime minister in Macdonald's cabinet. He agreed that Canada could absorb the $1-million debt and build a connecting railway within 10 years. The delegates were delighted.

But the package was a hard sell in both the Conservative caucus and then, once tabled, in the House of Commons. Again and again, opposition members pointed to the 10-year deadline. The United States, with 10 times the population, had scraped perilously deep to complete their coast-to-coast railway.

On Tuesday, March 28, 1871, Cartier rose to move the House into committee to "consider a series of resolutions respecting the admission of British Columbia into union with Canada." The proposed railway would not cost the public treasury more than $100-million, Cartier told the House. "But whatever it costs," he added, "I assure the House that there will be no more taxation on the country more than exists at present." He was soon seconded by a moving speech delivered by a Conservative backbencher.

▶ **DR. JAMES ALEXANDER GRANT** (Russell): I have listened with a very great degree of pleasure to the broad-spirited and statesmanlike observations of the hon. minister of militia and defence (Mr. Cartier). Truly, this is the age of union, in which we, as a people enjoying the fullest extent of freedom under the eye and protection of the Mother Country, should come together and realize the privileges of union in the widest and most comprehensive sense. These are the signs of the times. These are the signs by which four million of Her Majesty's subjects, scattered over this widespread country, recognize the importance of self-government with a warm allegiance to that Sovereign who, though distant, dwells in the homes and hearts of the people of this country.

An examination of the statistics of the population of British Columbia shows the somewhat remarkable fact that the male exceeds the female population by about 277 per cent! The wonder is that British Columbia should have attained its present prosperous condition wanting in so great a measure so material an element of success!

In 1863, British Columbia was looked upon as being in a flourishing condition, stimulated as it was to the utmost degree of intensity by the gold fever. After a time, things in general assumed a more normal state. Farms became cultivated, immense herds of cattle were raised, saw and grist mills were erected, and the lumberman's axe found its way into the magnificent forests. Material prosperity and general advancement are now taking the place of the feverish gold excitement, which is gradually passing away.

When we become possessors of British Columbia, we shall have a most magnificent inland sea of harbours such as between Vancouver and the mainland. It appears as if set apart by a special Providence as a depot for the shipping of the East, and as an entrance to the great highway for all nations across the British American continent. Doubtless, in course of time, the trade of China, Japan and the Asiatic Archipelago will centre there. This is the prize that was as anxiously sought after in ancient as it is in modern times. Persia, Assyria, Carthage and Rome prospered and held, in fact, commercial supremacy while they controlled the trade of the East.

This is the inheritance of the Pacific coast. What better or more substantial proof could we have than the expression of the sentiment which only a few days ago flashed across the Atlantic telegraph, that England would as soon think of having itself annexed to the United States as to allow any portion of this country to be attached to the neighbouring republic. Both England and the United States are equally well aware that the time has now arrived when that power that shall be enabled to construct the shortest route between Asia and Europe will hold the commercial supremacy of this continent in its grasp. The great trade of the East will not alone pass the Suez Canal and the Red Sea. This is the prize which we as a people must look forward to. I trust the day is near at hand when British Columbia will become part and parcel of the Dominion. ◄

The debate on first reading lasted seven hours, and the House adjourned at midnight. Over the next few days, several opposition objections were put to the House. "A reliable authority in British Columbia lately stated the population at 10,000 whites and 40,000 Indians," explained Alexander Galt, who, since his resignation as minister of finance in November of 1867, had joined the ranks of the opposition. "Aborigines should not be placed on an equal footing with the whites for the purposes of framing the financial basis of the Union, for revenue purposes at least." Alexander Mackenzie moved that the commitment upon Canada to complete the railway in 10 years be replaced by a simple pledge to survey and "to prosecute the route at as early a period as the state of its finances will justify."

One by one, the opposition amendments were conclusively defeated. On Saturday, April 1, 1871, Cartier moved second reading of the bill, and on July 20 British Columbia became the sixth province to enter the Canadian confederation.

A PARLIAMENT SOLD
►►►►►►►►►►►►►

THE 1872 ELECTION was not turning out according to Macdonald's predictions. The Tory campaign was plagued by financing difficulties. Macdonald could only watch with envy as a well-oiled Liberal organization poured a quarter of a million dollars into their campaign. Macdonald himself faced a hotly contested battle in his Kingston riding. Canadians, it seemed, were not as sure of his leadership as he had hoped.

Meanwhile, the Pacific Scandal was unfolding in Montreal, secretly at first. George-Etienne Cartier, fatally stricken with Bright's disease, had come under the domineering influence of Montrealer Sir Hugh Allan, the richest man in Canada. Allan and David Lewis Macpherson were locked in a fierce battle for control of the federal charter of the company to receive the contract for the construction of the Canadian Pacific railway. Allan had formed the Canadian Pacific Railway Company, and Macpherson, the Interoceanic Railway Company. Separately, they had begun to lobby Macdonald and his ministers. Macdonald responded by urging the two to cooperate and to merge the two corporate concerns. A deal was almost reached in the waning days of July 1873, when Macpherson travelled to Montreal to meet with Allan. The only remaining issue was the presidency of the merged corporation. Allan wanted the position. Macpherson insisted that the board of directors, once appointed, decide the matter. On July 26, Macdonald met

Macpherson in Kingston, and the prime minister was able to convince him to accept Allan at the helm.

But Allan was adept. Receiving Macdonald's assurances that "the power of the government will be exercised to secure him the position of president — the whole matter to be kept quiet until after the election," he decided to press for more concessions. He was well aware of the financial difficulties the Conservative party was experiencing, and no less aware of Cartier's difficulties in his riding of Montreal East (Cartier eventually lost). Allan demanded that his designates receive a majority of the stock and that, if negotiations with Macpherson were unsuccessful after two months, the charter for the building of Canada's national railway be given exclusively to the Canadian Pacific Railway Company. "Friends of the government will expect to be assisted with funds in the pending elections," he added, attaching a list of immediate payments to Macdonald, Cartier and Hector Langevin, the minister of public works.

Macdonald received the latest demands by telegram on July 31, the day before polling opened in Kingston. The 1872 election was the last federal election to be conducted over a period of several weeks, and some polls closed as late as September 3. Macdonald, preoccupied with salvaging his seat, replied angrily, repudiating Allan's suggestion. Allan agreed to withdraw the letter containing the disagreeable offer but left the $25,000 deposit in Macdonald's Merchants' Bank account. As the early August election returns began to enter, Macdonald watched in horror as the Liberals began racking up Commons seats. Allan's

deposit was quickly divvied: $2,000 went to Francis Hincks in a losing battle in South Brant, Ontario; $1,500 to John Carling in his attempt at election in London, Ontario, and to Rufus Stephenson in Kent. As if exhilarated by the propinquity of electoral victory, Macdonald threw caution to the wind. On August 26, he wired Allan's lawyer, John Abbott (the future prime minister), and delivered the document that would eventually fell him. "I must have another ten thousand dollars," the prime minister telegraphed. "Will be the last time of calling. Do not fail me."

A week later the final polls were in and Macdonald had himself a small majority. In total, Allan had given Macdonald $45,000. Cartier and Langevin had received $117,000. Sir Hugh Allan had bought himself a Parliament.

Still, the transactions with Allan remained the secret of a select few. In the speech from the throne, the government announced that it had "caused a charter to be granted to a body of Canadian capitalists for the construction of the Pacific Railway." But in the spring of 1873 rumours began to trickle out. As early as March 23, the Toronto *Globe* reported that Richard Potter, the president of the Grand Trunk Railway, had been approached for favours by Macdonald and Hincks. "We might have influenced eight or nine constituencies," recalled Potter, according to the *Globe*'s correspondent. With the appearance of outrage, Macdonald rose in the House to read a telegraphed message from Potter, that he "distinctly deny statement of Globe correspondent." The prime minister must have been terrified, but for the time being his secret held. Until April 2.

► **LUCIUS HUNTINGTON** (Shefford): Mr. Speaker, it was my duty to lay the statement I desire to make before the House at the earliest possible moment. From my place here, and under the strong sense of my responsibility as a member of this House, it of course becomes my duty to make the following motion:

> *A member of this House believes that he can establish by satisfactory evidence that in anticipation of the legislation of last session as to the Pacific Railway, an agreement was made between Sir Hugh Allan,*

acting for himself and other certain Canadian promoters, and George McMullen acting for certain United States capitalists, who, by the latter, agreed to furnish all the funds necessary for the construction of the railway, and to give the former a certain percentage of interest in consideration of their influence and position — the scheme agreed on being ostensibly that of a Canadian company, with Sir Hugh Allan at its head;

Subsequently, an understanding was come to between the government and Allan and John Abbott that Allan and his friends should advance a large sum of money for the purpose of aiding the elections of ministers and their supporters at the next general election and that he and his friends should receive the contract for the construction of the railway;

Accordingly, Allan did advance a large sum of money for the purpose mentioned, and at the solicitation and under the pressing instances of the ministers;

It is ordered that a committee of seven members be appointed to enquire into all the circumstances connected with the negotiations for the consideration of the Pacific Railway.

MR. SPEAKER — JAMES COCKBURN (Northumberland West): Shall this motion pass?
RIGHT HON. SIR JOHN A. MACDONALD — Prime Minister (Kingston): Lost!
SOME HON. MEMBERS: Carried!
MR. SPEAKER: Let the members be called in. ◄

Huntington's resolution was lost on a vote of 107 to 76. But Macdonald offered no explanation or denial of the sensational charges.

That night, government backbenchers began pressuring cabinet members for an enquiry. "We found a great deal of uneasiness among our friends," Macdonald wrote to Cartier, who was in London, England, consulting with medical specialists. "It looked like stifling an enquiry." The next day, Macdonald announced that he would table a government motion to appoint a special committee of five to investigate Huntington's charges. Immediately, controversy arose over procedural aspects of the proposed committee. Prorogation was pending, and there was clearly insufficient time for the committee to adequately investigate. Moreover, no act of Parliament existed empowering an ad hoc committee of the House to take evidence under oath.

One by one, led by Alexander Mackenzie, Liberal members challenged the prime minister on the committee's terms of reference. The resolution, it appeared, suffered from wanton lack of preparation, which Liberal members were not prepared to ascribe to accident. Macdonald acknowledged the opposition concerns but simply added that, alternatively, he was prepared to set up a royal commission if necessary. Mackenzie replied that a royal commission reported to the government, not to Parliament. Amidst legal confusion, the members were called in, and by ballot five members were appointed to the Pacific Railway committee. For the time being, the Huntington allegations were suppressed as the committee organized itself. As part of the compromise, Macdonald yielded to quick passage of an oaths bill, giving the committee the power to take evidence under oaths.

Other significant topics were dealt with in the First Session of the Second Parliament. Prince Edward Island was admitted into the union. Simultaneous membership in federal and provincial legislatures was prohibited. But the full attention of the country focused on the allegation of the member for Shefford and the coming proceedings of the committee.

THE DAY PARLIAMENT WAS GAGGED
▶▶▶▶▶▶▶▶▶▶▶▶▶▶▶▶▶▶▶▶▶▶▶▶▶▶

A FEW WEEKS AFTER the Pacific Railway committee was established, Lucius Huntington provided the chairman, John Cameron (Cardwell), with a list of witnesses and documents he intended to sub-poena. "When Macdonald saw the list," wrote Dale Thompson in *Clear Grit*, a biography of Alexander Mackenzie, "he knew the situation was serious."

Hugh Allan was in England, trying to secure financiers for the railway project. Macdonald appeared before the committee and requested a postponement of the hearings until July 2, to give Allan and the railway company's lawyer and Conservative member for Argenteuil, John Abbott, time to return from England.

The committee split on the prime minister's request, and the Conservative chairman cast the deciding vote in favour of postponement. On May 6, the committee's recommendation to postpone until July 2 was tabled before Parliament and caused a bitter exchange between Macdonald and Huntington. "The hon. gentleman has led me to show my hand as far as he will be able to do," shouted Huntington. "I will not be misled again. The hon. gentleman need not fancy that I have given them all."

Macdonald responded that all he had asked for was a postponement "till witnesses for the defence were ready." He then accused the member for Shefford of hiding in Montreal and failing to follow up on his charges before the committee. "The government is innocent of the charge, which I know is a foul calumny," Macdonald added. "The hon. gentleman has not sufficient grounds to make these charges. That is between God and him. The government denies *in toto* the charges. Neither by word, thought, deed nor action has the government done anything of which they could or ought to be ashamed of."

The sparring continued unabated between other members. The Hansard reporter noted that one member "on rising to address the House was interrupted by slamming of desks and other noises from the government benches." Another rose amidst "unseemly noises from the government benches."

The next day, it was announced that the House of Lords had disallowed the oaths bill as *ultra vires* the powers of Parliament. The disallowance was the first item of business of the ad hoc Pacific Railway committee meeting as it opened in Montreal on July 2. Chairman Cameron expressed his opinion that without the ability to take evidence under oath, the work of the committee should be suspended until the date at which Parliament was scheduled to reconvene: August 13. The two Liberal members, Edward Blake and Antoine-Aimé Dorion, fought the proposal but it carried 3–2.

Huntington was not to be outdone. On July 4, both the Montreal *Herald* and the Toronto *Globe* published some of the most incriminating letters. The second blow came on July 18. There, in print, were the prime minister's words to Abbott: ". . . must have another ten thousand. . . . Do not fail me." George Norris, Abbott's disgruntled clerk, had stolen the letters while Abbott was in England and sold them to Liberal leaders in Montreal.

Throughout the entire ordeal, Governor General the Earl of Dufferin had kept confidence in his prime minister. Dufferin and Macdonald were close friends, the prime minister becoming godfather to the Governor's Canadian-born daughter in May of 1873. But with the publication of the letters, Liberal leaders began to pressure Dufferin to withdraw his support from the Conservative government. George Brown, the old Grit patriarch and owner-publisher of the *Globe*, wrote to Mackenzie on July 21, "I can hardly believe that he will, but if we judge from his conduct in asking the drunk debauchee to be Godfather for his child, he can do a great deal."

Attention quickly focused on the resumption of Parliament scheduled for August 13. Mackenzie wanted debate and a vote of confidence. The Liberal House leader wrote no fewer than three letters to the members of his caucus insisting that they attend the House on August 13. Macdonald turned to his constant companion — gin. He disappeared from his Rivière-du-Loup summer residence for a few days of drinking in Lévis, Quebec, prompting, on August 4, the Montreal *Witness* to report: "Yesterday afternoon Sir John attempted to commit suicide by jumping from the wharf into the water. He was rescued but now lies, it is asserted, in a precarious condition."

"I never was better in my life," asserted Macdonald in a hurried dispatch to his family and friends. But in his drunken stupor, he had neglected to summon government members to Ottawa to meet the opposition offensive.

August 13 was the Earl of Dufferin's day. He arrived in the nation's capital by train from a Charlottetown vacation in the morning only to receive a message that Macdonald urgently wanted to see him. Macdonald presented him with a cabinet resolution requesting the prorogation of Parliament. He warned Dufferin that the Liberals had gathered all their members in the capital; more than enough to topple the government. Government members had not been requested to assemble in Ottawa, except enough to ensure quorum, as Macdonald had previously stated that Parliament would meet only *pro forma* and only for the purposes of receiving the Pacific Railway committee's report. Macdonald asked for the issuance of a royal commission to complete the work of the aborted committee.

Dufferin was under growing pressure from the Colonial Office in England to allow for "thorough and immediate investigation into the astonishing charges against the ministers." He demanded to meet with the cabinet to hear their advice directly. Macdonald left to arrange the meeting. Then Dufferin received another delegation. It was Richard Cartwright carrying a petition signed by 92 members, of which 12 were "ministerialists," or known supporters of the Macdonald ministry. The petition asked Dufferin "not to prorogue Parliament" until the House had given the Pacific Scandal a full hearing.

By 3 p.m., the opposition benches were full. The prime minister waited at the door of Parliament to greet the Governor General, as was the custom, as 35 nervous Tory members watched the army of more than 80 Grits assembled across the floor of the House. Mackenzie glanced nervously around. He spotted the Usher of the Black Rod just outside the door of the Green Chamber. For the Liberals, the key to forcing debate was to intervene at the moment between the Speaker's entry and that of the Black Rod, which would summon them to the Senate. Once there, they would be powerless to prevent prorogation. The Speaker entered the chamber.

▶ **ALEXANDER MACKENZIE** (Lambton): I propose to address you, Sir, and the House, upon a question of privilege! In the present grave circumstances under which we are called together, I feel it incumbent upon me to place this motion in your hands.

MR. SPEAKER — JAMES COCKBURN (Northumberland West): Order! Order!

SOME HON. MEMBERS: Privilege! Privilege!

MR. SPEAKER: The House is not in session until the doors are opened.

[At this point the Sergeant-at-Arms pushed the doors of the Commons chamber open.]

MR. MACKENZIE: Moved by Mr. Mackenzie, seconded by Mr.

Holton! That this House during the present session ordered an inquiry into certain grave charges in connection with the granting of the charter and the contract for the construction of the Pacific Railway, which, if true, seriously affect the official honour and integrity of His Excellency's advisers and the privileges and the independence of Parliament. The investigation thus ordered has not so far been proceeded with, owing to circumstances not anticipated when the inquiry was ordered! It is the imperative duty of this House at the earliest moment to take such steps as will secure a full Parliamentary inquiry. Constitutional usages require that charges of corruption against ministers of the Crown shall be investigated by Parliament, and that the assumption of that duty by any tribunal created by the executive would be a flagrant violation of the principles of this House! This House will regard as highly reprehensible any person who may presume to advise His Excellency to prorogue Parliament before it should have an opportunity of taking action in the premises, inasmuch as such prorogation would render abortive all the steps taken up to the present time, would inflict an unprecedented indignity on Parliament and produce great dissatisfaction in the country!

[Three knocks being heard, the Sergeant-at-Arms announced that a messenger had arrived from the Senate.]

MR. SPEAKER: The message must be read!

MR. MACKENZIE: No message shall interrupt me! I stand here representing a constituency in this province and, I have reason to believe, the opinion of a very large number of people throughout the country! I propose to call the attention of the House to circumstances affecting the independence of Parliament!

USHER OF THE BLACK ROD: I am commanded by His Excellency the Governor General to acquaint this House that it is the pleasure of His Excellency that the members thereof do forthwith attend him in the Senate Chamber!

MR. MACKENZIE: There is nothing in the circumstances which justify His Excellency to prorogue Parliament for the purpose of protecting an accused ministry and I propose to proceed with the discussion of this matter! I have placed this motion in your hands because I have heard it is the intention to prorogue this House! ◄

But it was over. The Usher of the Black Rod, after shouting his summons, turned and walked out the door, Speaker Cockburn and government members in close tow. Before he knew it, Mackenzie and his Liberal caucus were alone in the chamber. They refused to attend the Senate ceremony and quickly convened in the Railway Committee Room. There, they took turns admonishing Cockburn, Macdonald, Dufferin, Abbott and Allan.

The next day, a royal commission was appointed by the Governor General, consisting of three judges. Dufferin sent for Mackenzie and explained that he was forced to take the advice of his constitutional advisers, the cabinet. It was little consolation. But within twelve weeks, the member for Lambton would receive another summons from Rideau Hall, and then it would be an offer to form the government of the Dominion of Canada.

THE FINAL CURTAIN
►►►►►►►►►►►►

ALTHOUGH LUCIUS Huntington declined to attend the sittings of the royal commission investigating the Pacific Scandal, the evidence it uncovered was sensational. Macdonald acted before the commission as counsel for the government. His desperate case would insist that the Allan money was in no way associated with the charter for the railway company; and besides, he had promised only the presidency. Campaign contributions, after all, were legal. The prime minister also held the portfolio of minister of justice. He hoped to cross-examine Huntington, especially to review the procurement of the telegrams. Huntington declined the commissioners' offer to examine the witnesses on his list. Instead, he declared that he would participate only in a forum of the House of Commons. Macdonald also faced the flight of George Norris, whom he dearly wanted to cross-examine in order to expose the methods of the Liberals. His last desperate strategy involved a conviction of theft against Norris, which would expose the Liberal to the charge of dealing with criminals and detract from the prime minister's own conduct. Before he could do so, though, Norris fled to the United States. When he did return to Montreal, Macdonald decided not to prosecute. That left Hugh Allan. He was called before the commission and admitted that he provided more than $162,600 to the Tory 1873 election coffers.

Incredibly, Dufferin stood by his First Minister. "As I said to you in very early days," wrote the Governor General to Macdonald on September 12, "I am convinced that you will come out entirely exonerated from the atrocious charges."

On October 23, Parliament reconvened and the Governor General received the report of the commissioners. The three judges declined to provide "an expression of their opinions upon the evidence" but tabled the evidence before the House. It was enough, pregnant with incriminating admissions of all sorts from Allan. Macdonald later reflected, "The imprudence of Sir Hugh in this whole matter has almost amounted to insanity."

Still, Macdonald hung on to the premiership, hoping even yet for a turn of public opinion against those telegram-stealing Grits. It was not to be. The throne speech referred to the report and evidence as deserving "careful attention." "It will be for you to determine whether it can be of any assistance to you," Dufferin told a packed Senate chamber. Members were also informed that the Canadian Pacific Railway Company had surrendered its charter. Allan had failed to secure sufficient European financing for the project; telegraphic reports of the scandal in Canada had greatly hindered his efforts.

As soon as the last speech on the address ended, Alexander Mackenzie rose and gave a long speech, reviewing as had so many members before him, and so many more would after him, his own interpretation of the events of the summers of 1872 and 1873. He closed his remarks with a motion: "That we have to acquaint His Excellency that by their course in reference to the investigation of the charges preferred by Mr. Huntington, in his place in this House, and under the facts disclosed in the evidence laid before us, His Excellency's advisers have merited the censure of this House." The countdown leading to the end of the Macdonald government had begun, even though, to a packed public gallery, on November 3, 1873, Sir John A. Macdonald offered one of the most powerful speeches of his political career.

▶ **RIGHT HON. SIR JOHN A. MACDONALD** — Prime Minister (Kingston): Mr. Speaker, the government never gave Sir Hugh Allan any contract that I am aware of. We never gave him any contract in which he had a controlling influence. We provided that not one of the board should hold more than $100,000 of the stock; that not one single man should have any interest in the contract whatever.

I put it to your own minds. There were thirteen men — Sir Hugh Allan and others incorporated by that charter. That charter — study it, take it home with you. Is there any single power, privilege or advantage given to Sir Hugh Allan with that contract that has not been given equally to the other twelve? It is not pretended that any of the other twelve paid money for their positions. It is not contended that the gentlemen gave anything further than their own personal feelings might dictate. You cannot name a man of these thirteen that has got an advantage over the other, except that Sir Hugh Allan has his name down first on the paper.

Can anyone believe that the government is guilty of the charges made against them? I call upon anyone who does to read that charter. Is there anything in that charter? If there is a word in that charter which derogates from the rights of Canada; if there is any undue privilege or right or preponderance given to anyone of these thirteen gentlemen, I say, Mr. Speaker, I am condemned. But, Sir, I commit myself, the government commits itself to the hands of the House; and far beyond this House, it commits itself to the country at large. We have faithfully done our duty. We have fought the battle of Union. We have had party strife setting province against province. And more than all, we have had in the greatest province, the preponderating province of the Dominion, every prejudice and sectional feeling that could be arrayed against us.

I have been the victim of that conduct to a great extent. But I have fought the battle of Confederation, the battle of Union, the battle of the Dominion of Canada. I throw myself upon this House. I throw myself upon this country. I throw myself upon posterity, and I know that notwithstanding the many failings of my life, I shall have the voice of this country and this House rallying around me. And, Sir, if I am mistaken in that, I can confidently appeal to a higher court — to the court of my own conscience, and to the court of posterity.

I leave it to this House with every confidence. I am equal to either fortune. ◄

It was too little, too late. Macdonald sat down and was followed by Edward Blake. Blake, much to the chagrin of all members, proceeded with his customary monotone drone. He matched and surpassed Macdonald's five-and-a-half-hour speech. Once he did conclude, the House's attention turned to two non-partisan newcomers. David Laird, the member from Queen's, PEI announced his intention to vote against the government. Then, the Speaker asked: "Are the members ready for the question?" Donald Smith, the member from Selkirk, Manitoba rose. His support for the government could yet tilt the balance. Smith started slowly and brought on great cheers from the government side when he mentioned that he "felt that the leader of the government (Mr. Macdonald) was incapable of taking money from Allan for corrupt purposes." When he added that he would be most willing to vote for the government motion, the government side let out wild cheers. According to Smith's biographer, W.T.R. Preston, the Tory whip led a contingent of government members to the House restaurant, where "they filled their glasses to the health of Donald A." Smith allowed the disturbance to subside before he completed his sentence: ". . . could I do so conscientiously. It is with very great regret that I feel I can not do so. For the honour of the country, no government should exist that has a shadow of a suspicion of this kind resting on them." Minutes later, at 1:30 a.m., the House adjourned.

On Wednesday, November 5, 1873, Sir John A. Macdonald visited the Governor General and offered the resignation of his government. Dufferin was all too relieved to accept it. They shook hands and Macdonald went to the Parliament Buildings. At 3 p.m., the House resumed. Now just a member of the House, John A. Macdonald rose and announced that the ministry had resigned. "His Excellency has sent for Mr. Mackenzie to form an administration," he said to loud cheers from the opposition benches. He moved for an adjournment.

By the next day, the sitting arrangement in the House had been reversed. Macdonald, Tupper, Langevin and Bowell occupied the front rows of the opposition benches, on the Speaker's left. Minutes later, the Second Parliament of the government of Canada was prorogued by the Earl of Dufferin. Mackenzie called a general election and was returned with a 133–73 majority.

3
Transitions
▶▶▶▶▶▶▶▶▶▶▶▶▶▶

COUP D'ETAT
▶▶▶▶▶▶▶▶

LUC LETELLIER DE ST.-JUST was described in a biography of Alexander Mackenzie, written by William Buckingham and George William Ross, as a "radical of radicals — jealous in honour, sudden and quick in quarrel"; a most questionable candidate for as sensitive a position as lieutenant-governor. Minister of agriculture in Mackenzie's first cabinet, Letellier was appointed lieutenant-governor of Quebec in December 1876. Less than 16 months later, his actions would cause one of the greatest constitutional crises Canada has ever known.

Letellier took residence in Quebec City and was presented to the premier, Charles de Boucherville. De Boucherville was a Tory. Any doubts of the dislike between the two political parties within the *belle province* were confirmed when Mackenzie travelled to the provincial capital in June of 1876 to attend a function hosted by Letellier's predecessor. Upon learning that the Liberal prime minister was to be present, de Boucherville and his entire cabinet withdrew their acceptances to attend.

In 1876, responsible government — where elected officials govern, and representatives of Her Majesty such as lieutenant-governors follow the advice of elected ministers — was still in its formative years. The exact limits of representatives' residual powers were still uncertain. Premier de Boucherville, for example, neglected to advise Letellier in advance of bills being tabled in the national assembly.

On March 1, 1878, only days before the end of the provincial legislative session and royal assent to bills, Letellier had a note delivered to the premier. De Boucherville, with a 23-member majority in the Assembly, read that Letellier was dismissing him from the premiership! Letellier called upon the Liberal leader of the opposition, Henri Joly, to form a new government. Unfortunately, the lieutenant-governor had dismissed de Boucherville before the supply bill had passed through the assembly, and Joly found the provincial treasury empty. In addition, the Conservative majority quickly passed a non-confidence vote against the new premier. Letellier had forced a provincial election, which was scheduled for May 1.

A resolution from the Quebec National Assembly was read in the House of Commons on March 22 calling the dismissal of de Boucherville "an abuse of power in contempt of the majority of this House, whose confidence they possess, and still possess, and is a violation of the liberties and will of the people." Editorials appeared daily in the national press, most disapproving of Letellier's move. But still, no official reaction from Prime Minister Mackenzie. Until April 11, 1878.

Ironically, it was just after Mackenzie had risen to pay tribute to the departing Governor General of Canada, the Earl of Dufferin, that the leader of the opposition decided to force the prime minister's hand on the lieutenant-governor's action. Macdonald, always the wily politician, decided to see what mileage could be obtained in the House of Commons.

Criticism of Imperial representatives was a politically dangerous venture. One inappropriate or heavy-handed remark could spark an outcry from the Imperialist Canadian press and eliminate thousands of votes. But a well-presented case against the action of a lieutenant-governor, one which defended Canadian sovereignty, and one with the potential of isolating Quebec members of the government on the wrong side of an issue so dear to their constituents, was too strong a temptation — especially on the eve of a federal election.

▶ **SIR JOHN A. MACDONALD** — Leader of the Opposition (Kingston): Mr. Speaker, I move that the recent dismissal by the Lieutenant-Governor of Quebec of his ministers was unwise and subversive. A bad precedent is a dangerous thing, especially when we are in the commencement of our history. A flaw, a disease at the roots of the young tree, is surely to lead to early decay and, therefore, it is especially our duty to see that the tree planted by us shall be sheltered from every possible disease or infirmity which might destroy its value. If there is a mistake in administration: that can be cured by a change of government or of policy. If there is bad legislation: that can be cured by repealing or amending the objectionable act. But a precedent, once established, always has its influence. It is of the very greatest consequence, on this, the very first occasion when a great constitutional question has arisen, that we should deal with it in a manner worthy of it.

I had thought that at this time, in the nineteenth century, a question of this kind could not have arisen in Canada. It shows that eternal vigilance is the price of liberty.

I would call your attention to the act of the Lieutenant-Governor in the province of Quebec. It was a *coup d'état*. It was an outrage on the constitution. It was an outrage on free institutions and, above all, on British institutions and as such, was both unwise and unconstitutional.

Here we are, just before a general election in which there is to be a struggle of considerable, perhaps, of extreme warmth, from one end of the country to the other. It is alleged that Mr. Letellier was a partisan of the present government. He had before been one of its ministers. It is alleged that he allowed a ministry having the confidence of both Houses, to carry their measures almost to the end and, at the last moment, when he thought the legislation was complete, he sent them adrift and brought in new men belonging to the same political party as himself, and that all this was done for the purpose of getting hold of power in the province. This is a widely spread charge, be it untrue or be it true. The very fact of this done by the Lieutenant-Governor must have been obvious to him, and to any man of common sense, that it would be liable to do, has given rise to that charge, to that imputation, to that suspicion. It tended to show that the government did not exhibit the greatest of discretion in choosing him for that office.

I have made no attack. God forbid that I should do so for as yet I know not that the present ministry, at the head of which is the hon. member for Lambton, is liable to the charge, liable to attack, or liable to censure for anything which has taken place. And yet I do not know this and, therefore, I will not say it. But it depends upon that hon. gentleman to say whether he, the distinguished leader of the Liberal party of the country will — but I do not believe that the hon. gentleman will — sacrifice those great principles. I do not believe that that hon. gentleman will turn his back upon those principles which he has so long professed, and which have been his chief credit, the chief honour of his party. Mr. Speaker, I move the resolution. ◀

Mackenzie rose next. The long day was dragging into early evening. The prime minister rebutted that while a discussion of the actions of a lieutenant-governor was in order, any censure of an appointee of the Imperial government should occur only in the Imperial parliament. Mackenzie added that an election was in progress in Quebec, and that the judgement of Letellier's action should be left to the people. Quebec backbenchers joined the fray led by Louis Masson, the Conservative member for Terrebonne. "A great question has been raised in the province of Quebec," stated Masson, in support of his leader's motion. "The whole of our system of government depends on it."

Wilfrid Laurier, the 34-year-old minister of inland revenue and Liberal member for Quebec East, chastised Masson. "It is not our duty to criticize the conduct of Mr. Letellier," said Laurier. "I will not follow the hon. gentleman in controversy but will leave it to the judgement of the people." Edward Brooks, the Liberal member for Sherbrooke, followed with a speech that lasted for hours. Finally, as the clock struck 2 a.m., Brooks concluded: "If the Lieutenant-Governor of one of our provinces were permitted to do what neither the Sovereign nor the Governor General would venture to do, there would be no safety and no peace in the Dominion. *Could great men thunder, as Jove himself can. Jove would never be quiet! For every pelting petty officer would use his heaven or thunder! Nothing but thunder.*" After that literary quotation, the member for Charlevoix, Hector Langevin, moved adjournment.

The next day, debate began with a single question on the Pacific Railway project for the government, and the Quebec Crisis debate resumed in earnest. Hector Langevin led off, and went on for hours in damnation of Letellier. There was no more mincing words. Langevin called Letellier "a traitor to his race! A traitor to our beloved country!"

From all corners of the House, members rose to speak. A motion for adjournment was denied by the government benches; if the opposition wanted to drag on this debate, there would be no recess. The clock ticked on. Eventually, even the Hansard stenographer lost patience. When Josiah Plumb, the Conservative member for Niagara, began to read long legal texts, the report of the debates merely mentions that "Mr. Plumb quoted copiously from eminent authorities in support of his view that the Lieutenant-Governor had exceeded his constitutional functions." Plumb would not be the only speaker to have his long, windy speech short-quoted in Hansard.

Behind the curtains of the House, in the members' lobbies, both leaders were conferring with their colleagues. Macdonald was distributing to his members the names of various authorities to quote. The Conservatives were determined to talk this out, even if it meant filibustering until daybreak. And, indeed, alcoholic stimulants were in order!

From that point on, the House was completely out of control. Hansard gives some hint of the folly. On the record, Conservative Marie-Honorius-Ernest Cimon (Chicoutimi-Saguenay) remarked, "The noises made by hon. members opposite were their cries of conscience. There are strangers in the House. I think that the Speaker should redress the disorder or leave the chair!"

Speaker Timothy Anglin replied: "I will discharge my duty as I think it ought to be discharged. I have again and again appealed to hon. members to try and conduct the debate in a quiet and proper manner. I now appeal to hon. gentlemen on both sides to come to an arrangement and put an end to what I must regard as a most unseemly style of proceeding."

That was classic understatement. Unwritten in the transcript was an entire evening of outrageous breaches of parliamentary decorum. Emerson Bristol Biggar in *An Anecdotal Life of Sir John A. Macdonald* described the scene: "Members hammered at desks, blew on tin trumpets, imitated the crowing of cocks, sent up toy balloons, threw sand-crackers and hurled blue-books across the House. Once in a while amid the din some member would start up the Marseillaise, God Save the Queen or some plantation melody, and then the whole House would join in the song. There were always enough members to keep up the fun. The exhausted figures of some members would be found reclining on their desks, quite unconscious of the paper missiles being pelted at them. Mr. Mackenzie sometimes exhibited a face as long as a family churn, and sometimes was beaming with goodwill. Mr. Blake kept himself amused and awake by performing some extraordinary finger-music on his

desk. Once when Mr. Plumb was speaking, Samuel McDonnell of Inverness, with mock gravity, called the attention of the speaker to the fact that the member for Niagara was interrupting the music!"

Finally, at 6:05 a.m., Mackenzie and Macdonald agreed to a ceasefire. Mackenzie allowed an adjournment and Macdonald's motion was postponed to the following Monday. It was later defeated 112–70.

Prime Minister Mackenzie returned to his office and managed to write to George Brown. "John A. got very drunk early this morning and they had to get him stowed somewhere. I never saw such a scene with whisky before."

Incredibly, the House had not witnessed the end of the Tory

disruption of the last days of the Fifth Session of the Third Parliament. On Friday, May 10, 1878, just as the members were preparing for prorogation, the Speaker recognized Donald Smith, the member for Selkirk, on a question of privilege. Smith referred to a quote of Macdonald and Charles Tupper reported in the *Free Press*, insinuating that the Liberal administration had rewarded Smith for his "servile support" by trying to award his company with a railway contract. When Tupper retorted that Smith had asked for a cabinet position in 1873 in exchange for his vote during the Pacific Scandal, all hell broke loose.

► **CHARLES TUPPER** (Cumberland, Nova Scotia): Mr. Speaker, I rise to a question of order. The hon. gentleman has had that speech here during the three months that we have been in session, and to speak at the moment when Black Rod is coming to the door and thus to shelter himself from the answer which he would otherwise get . . .

MR. MACDONALD: And the punishment he would otherwise get.

MR. TUPPER: A more cowardly thing I have never seen ventured on in this House.

DONALD SMITH (Selkirk): The charge of being a coward I throw back on the hon. gentleman.

MR. MACDONALD: Let the poor man go.

MR. SMITH: I never asked, prayed for or got a favour from the last government.

MR. TUPPER: The hon. gentleman begged of me to implore the leader of the government to make him a member of the Privy Council. That is what he asked for and he was refused.

MR. SMITH: The hon. gentleman knows that he states what is wholly untrue and, driven to wit's end, is now going back to a journey he and I made to the Northwest in 1869. I give the most positive denial to any assertion made by him, or any other person, that I asked for any favour from the government.

THE SERGEANT-AT-ARMS: Mr. Speaker, a message from His Excellency the Governor General.

MR. SPEAKER — TIMOTHY ANGLIN (Gloucester, New Brunswick): I have very much the pleasure in informing the House that it now becomes my duty to receive the messenger . . .

MR. SMITH: He knows . . .

MR. TUPPER: Coward! Coward! Sit down! Coward! Coward! Coward!

MR. SPEAKER: I . . .

MR. SMITH: You are the coward! The day after that 4th of November, who came to me with a proposition to throw over the right hon. gentleman and the present member for Charlevoix (Hector Langevin) if I would consent to give up the position I had deemed it my duty to take in the House the evening before?

MR. TUPPER: Mean, treacherous coward!

MR. SMITH: Who is the coward? The House will decide! It is yourself!

MR. SPEAKER: Admit the messenger!

MR. MACDONALD: That fellow Smith is the biggest liar I ever met! ◄

On Macdonald's words, the messenger was admitted and read the summons to the Senate. As the members rose, Macdonald and Tupper tried to reach Smith, and for a moment it appeared as though a brawl might break out. "I can lick you, Smith, faster'n hell can scorch a feather," Macdonald yelled. But the Sergeant-at-Arms, assisted by Liberal Joe Rymal (South Wentworth) and other volunteers, managed to separate the belligerents before they came to blows. According to W.T.R. Preston, the Speaker tried to lead the procession out of the Commons chamber. "After the cabinet followed as excited a mob as ever disgraced the floor of a parliamentary chamber. Angry Tories, with arms uplifted as if to strike, pushed towards the object of their hatred. The crowd swayed to and fro." One opposition member managed to hit Smith's hat off. Once in the Senate chamber, the agitation quickly subsided. Donald Smith later described the experience as one of the most exciting in his life.

Macdonald won the 1878 general election and went on to serve as prime minister for 13 consecutive years, until his death in 1891.

THE SECRET SERVICE AND RIEL
▶▶▶▶▶▶▶▶▶▶▶▶▶▶▶▶▶

WHEN PRIME MINISTER Sir John A. Macdonald completed his lecture on March 26, 1885, opposition member Richard Cartwright remarked, "Those of us who have had the pleasure of sitting in the House for any length of time with the First Minister are tolerably aware that the justice of his cause is always in inverse ratio to the violence of his declamation." This may well have been the case. What was more certain, however, was that the young history of Canada was held precariously in the balance.

Much had changed since the days of the 1870 rebellion. Telegraph lines now stretched across the prairies. The last spike of the Canadian Pacific Railway would be driven into the soil at Craigellachie, British Columbia, in only seven months.

But then, from the recent past of Canada, reappeared Louis Riel. On March 23, 1885, Macdonald informed the House that "a number of half-breeds, led by Riel, have cut the [telegraph] wires between Qu'Appelle and the crossing of the south branch of the Saskatchewan."

On Thursday, March 26, under further questioning from Edward Blake, the leader of the opposition, Macdonald released a few sparse facts. Yes, there was a movement of troops and yes, there had been some difficulties with Métis land claims in the territory known as the Northwest (now Saskatchewan and Alberta).

Macdonald explained that the troubles were caused by a misunderstanding of surveyors who had carved square lots, chopping out whole parts of irregularly shaped land occupied by Métis. In addition, Macdonald informed the House, a number of Métis had sold their 240-acre scrips of land in Manitoba. "Having squandered the land they got in Manitoba, saying 'one Métis looks like another, the government will never know it,' they claimed the land again."

But Blake rose again and began a lengthy condemnation of the Conservative government's handling of the uprising. Referring first to the recent claims of a member that land-grabbing was rampant in the Northwest, Blake claimed he could "find influential members of Parliament who have made applications [for land grants]; that there was the carcass at which the eagles that follow in the wake of the government were gathered; that everybody and his son-in-law or his friend or his ally should have a suitable timber limit or mine." Blake followed this with the most sensational part of his speech, accusing Macdonald of "handing [Riel] secret service money, $1,000 to pay his expenses when he was out of the country."

► **RIGHT HON. SIR JOHN A. MACDONALD** — Prime Minister (Carleton): Mr. Speaker, there has been rising after rising in the United States. Sir, there has not been one single blow struck in anger in our Northwest until this thing happened the other day [March 23].

You must recollect that that country is occupied by savages, or semi-savages, by men who are now driven to desperation through the disappearance of their only means of procuring food. And hungry men are desperate. Look back at Hansard and you will find that when I came forward here and asked for votes to support these poor people, we were taunted across the floor. I stated that the buffalo had disappeared, the game they depended on for support; they were surrounded by whites; they were crowded out of their country — and yet we were told about the lavish expenditures of this extravagant government.

We kept them on short rations. We tried to force them — I am speaking now of the Indians — and we have forced them upon their reserves. By slow degrees, we are introducing among them the habits of cultivation. The course taken towards the Métis has been kind, paternal, and in every way for the purpose of forwarding their best interests.

But, oh, says the hon. gentleman, there has been apathy in this matter! These people have been driven to desperation! These people would not have sent for Riel if the sense of injustice, if the denial of justice had not forced them to take this extraordinary step!

If the hon. gentleman waits until the Indian or half-breed ceases to grumble, he will have to wait till the day of doom. They always grumble. If you give an Indian four pounds of pork, and it is two pounds more than he is entitled to, he will grumble because he does not get six. And the half-breed has all the acquisitiveness of the Indian and the strong desire to press his claims of the white man.

The hon. gentleman wants to know what we will do with Riel. Why, Mr. Speaker, the hon. gentleman offered $5,000 to try and catch him! $5,000 was offered for this traitor and murderer and it never was paid. I made a speech at Peterborough saying I wished to God we could catch Riel. There never was a prayer more sincerely offered. If we had got Riel he would have been brought and tried. If he had been brought down here we could have got a conviction against him, and the consequences of conviction would have followed. We tried to arrest him, and the hon. gentleman sought to help us by offering the reward. But it was offered so loudly, it was trumpeted abroad so strongly, that the man ran away. I leave it to this House, and I leave it to the sober judgement of this country, whether it will be said that what I did was done to promote peace and prosperity. ◄

Even as the prime minister was speaking, Superintendent Lief Crozier, in charge of the Mounted Police detachment at Battleford, had set out for Duck Lake with a hundred mounted men, most of whom were deputized citizens of Prince Albert. Imprudently, Crozier did not wait for reinforcements arriving from Prince Albert. The night before, Riel's men had looted the public store in the small Métis community situated halfway between Batoche and Carlton.

THE 48-DAY REBELLION
►►►►►►►►►►►►►

EVERYTHING CHANGED on March 26, 1885. The prime minister interrupted routine proceedings in the early evening to solemnly read a telegram he had received from Commissioner Colonel Irvine. "Were met by some 200 rebels," wrote Irvine. "Rebels fired first. Crozier retreated. Ten civilians of Prince Albert and two policemen killed." Macdonald then informed the House that now that bullets had been fired, the House would receive "the fullest information."

According to the latest intelligence, Riel had 1,500 men and six cannons. Later that evening, the minister of militia and defence, Sir Adolphe Caron, told the House that 800 troops were being readied for immediate deployment to the North-west. With all but 70 miles of the distance separating Ottawa from the insurgents covered by railway track, it would not be long for the Canadian militia to reach the front, in what would be the first important use of the Canadian Pacific Railway, then under construction. Their commanding officer, Maj.-Gen. Frederick Middleton, was already in Winnipeg.

Riel realized that he had passed the point of no return. His initial success at Duck Lake brought him enthusiastic reinforcements from Métis settlements and Sioux from White Cap's band as well as a number of Cree warriors.

Daily in the House of Commons questions were asked of the government. For once, the information was readily provided, offering a day-by-day account of the progress of the military operation, one that would last 48 days. The reading of telegrams must have been dramatic in an age that could not even dream of radio or TV.

► *March 30*

RIGHT HON. SIR JOHN A. MACDONALD — Prime Minister (Carleton): The militia and military men are moving on from Ontario westward. There is no fear that they may be involved in trouble with the Indians. . . .

There is one exception I nearly forgot. A telegram has arrived that an Indian well known as troublesome, Poundmaker, and Little Pine have donned war paint not far from Battleford and have some men with them.

ALEXANDER ROBERTSON (West Hastings): I ask whether the mounted police have been provided with Gatling guns. Those guns have been found to be very valuable in the Egyptian war. As they will fire 100 shots in a few minutes, they would be found, I think, very valuable in the Northwest.

SIR ADOLPHE CARON — Minister of Militia and Defence (Quebec County): Gatling guns have been ordered. I do not consider it advisable to indicate more explicitly what measures have been taken to provide them with arms and ammunition. ◄

Thousands of miles west of the debating chamber of the Parliament of Canada, Major-General Middleton was organizing his army in Fort Qu'Appelle when, without warning on April 2, Cree of Big Bear's band attacked and massacred eight settlers in the small settlement of Frog Lake.

Riel was in Batoche, hoping that a Canadian delegate would soon call, as they had so promptly in 1870. He had no hand in the Frog Lake massacre, but once it occurred, he decided to make the best of it and sent runners to the neighbouring reserves, urging the Natives to join the Métis army amassing in Batoche. He was not ignorant of the commotion he was causing in eastern Canada, even though, because of the sabotage of telegram lines and the isolation of the Frog Lake settlement, members of the House of Commons were not made aware of the tragedy until eight days later.

► *April 10*

MR. MACDONALD: A telegram has been received from Mr. Dickens who commands the Mounted Police at Fort Pitt:

> *There was a massacre at Frog Lake. The following were killed: T.T. Quinn, Indian agent, a half-breed; James Delaney, farm instructor; Mr. Gowanlock and wife; Rev. Father Forfar, a priest; Father Lemarchand, a priest, and two other men — I believe they were lay brethren. Mrs. Delaney is a prisoner. H. Quinn, nephew of the Quinn who was murdered, escaped and arrived here yesterday.*

April 13

MR. MACDONALD: I may as well inform the House that Mr. Dewdney, the Lieutenant-Governor, accompanied by Father Lacombe, missionary to the Blackfeet, have held a meeting with the Blackfeet, headed by their chief, Crowfoot. I have received a telegram which I will read:

> *Blackfoot Crossing, 11th April, 1885*
> *On behalf of myself and people I wish to send through you to the Great Mother the words I have given to the Governor at a council held at which all my minor chiefs and young men were present. We are agreed and determined to remain loyal to the Queen. Our young men will go to work on their reserves and will raise all the crops we can. Continued reports and many lies are brought to us, and we don't know what to believe. But now that we have seen the Governor and heard him speak, we will shut our ears and only listen to and believe what is told us through the Governor. Should any Indians come to our reserve and ask us to join them in war we will send them away. We have asked for nothing but the Governor has given us a little present of tea and tobacco. He will tell*

*you what other talk we had at our council. It was all good — not one
bad word.*

Crowfoot ◄

Fort Qu'Appelle was 255 miles from Batoche. Riel's military
adviser and confidant, Gabriel Dumont, was aware that Middleton had begun moving north from Fort Qu'Appelle with 600
troops, but he did not believe that they would succeed in
making much progress on the drenched spring prairie grass-
lands.

► *April 20*

MR. CARON: Before the orders of the day are called, I desire to read
to the House two telegrams. The first is dated at Clarke's Crossing,
the 17th, and is from Major-General Middleton:

*Men have behaved and marched wonderfully. 198 miles from Fort
Qu'Appelle in 11 days, in this country and weather, is a feat not to be
despised. The hardships have been real and great and have been borne
by all ranks, not only without a murmur, but cheerfully.* ◄

Parliament was bracing itself for confrontation. Middleton was
now camped at Clarke's Crossing, only 50 miles south along the
Saskatchewan River from Batoche. On April 23, his troops
broke camp and again moved north. Middleton split his troops,
sending 550 up the east bank, the remainder along the west
bank. When Dumont heard of the soldiers' movement from the
Métis scouts, he quickly devised an ambush: they would surprise the Canadians as they dropped into the Fish Creek ravine,
which cut the trail as it flowed west into the Saskatchewan. Riel,
Dumont and 180 men sped on horseback to Fish Creek.

That night, as they set camp, two of their men arrived with
news that another Canadian battalion was marching towards
Batoche from the east. Although the rumour would later prove
false, Riel and 50 men returned immediately to Batoche.

The next morning, the Métis riflemen arrived at the Fish
Creek ravine and began digging rifle pits. Sharpshooters were
positioned. Suddenly, a group of Middleton's mounted scouts

reared around the bend. A shot rang out, and the battle of Fish
Creek began.

► *April 24*

SIMON DAWSON (Algoma): I understand that very important news
has been received from the Northwest. Would it not be well that it
should be read to the House so that all may hear it.

MR. SPEAKER — GEORGE KIRKPATRICK (Frontenac):

Winnipeg, April 24
Fight began at 9:15 a.m. Rebels advancing from coulee, near river,
opened fire upon scouts led by Major Boulton. Latter returning fire when
rebels mounted and retired to place of ambush. From ambush they rose
each time in firing. General Middleton at once deployed troops in
skirmishing order. "A" Battery could not at first feel enemy with guns,
so good were their shelter. Eventually, however, battery got into better
position and rained raking fire among them. Two houses in which rebels
reserves were secluded were demolished. Rebels next made dash and fought
90th at close quarters but severe fire from left wing forced rebels to retire.
Fight was Indian style on part of rebels who were always concealed
behind trees or in bluffs. Their fire was hot and very effective. Captain
Clark with sharpshooters first advanced in skirmishing order after scouts
signalled danger, and closely following were Toronto School of Infantry,
latter taking right flank. Conflict now became general and terribly
severe. Indians were exceedingly combative and war-whoop yells could be
heard distinctly some distance off. They rallied time and time again,
keeping up incessant fire for fully an hour. Subsequently fire slackened
on part of enemy but was again resumed shortly after noon. Prairie was
set on fire as result of battle but heavy rain which set in about noon
quenched it. Party of rebels have been successfully driven from ambush,
in ravine, by hard firing by volunteers. General Middleton had close
call, being shot through hat.

Battle field, N.W.T. ◄

The Métis had been badly beaten. Casualties and desertions
were so high that Dumont soon found himself with only 50 men.
Unmentioned in the telegram was that Middleton had not
ordered a third charge, as Dumont lay huddled deep in the

ravine doubting if his men could resist another charge. In hopelessness, they sang old French war songs and yelled taunts at the French-Canadians they knew were among Middleton's ranks. Then, just as they realized that the Canadians were actually retreating, Métis reinforcements returned from Batoche. That evening, under the cover of darkness, Dumont and his men left their rifle pits and retreated to Batoche. But Middleton and his Canadian army were now but 13 miles from their headquarters.

A hundred miles across the prairie plains, 375 other Canadian troops marched into Battleford on April 29, putting an end to harassment from the nearby reserve under the control of Chief Poundmaker. On May 2, Colonel Otter, in command of the Dominion troops, made the foolhardy decision to attack.

► *May 6*

MR. MACDONALD: I have just received a telegram from Superintendent Herchmer, who commanded the Mounted Police with Colonel Otter:

> *Battleford, May 3rd, received at Ottawa, May 6th*
> *Column fought Poundmaker for seven hours and demolished his camp. Police behaved beyond praise, receiving first fire, holding position while column formed for attack and remaining there throughout engagement. Total loss: eight killed, fifteen wounded. Moved eighty miles in thirty hours, seven of which were fighting. Enemies killed and wounded: fully one hundred.* ◄

But later reports proved that the telegram was not accurate. In fact, the Canadians suffered more casualties than did the Indians. While the reserve had sustained severe damage, it had not been overrun. Otter had been forced to retreat. Chief Poundmaker saddled and rode for Batoche.

On May 7, Middleton began the final march to Batoche, in command of 1,000 soldiers. Riel and Dumont had 250 men. The rebels dug rifle pits around their village. On the ninth, prisoners were locked in the basement of the general store for their safety. Middleton appeared near the village church and the first shots of combat were fired. Twice on that first day, Middleton ordered his men to charge; twice they were repelled. When the sun set, the Canadians retreated to a temporary camp, having suffered three casualties. None of Riel's men were killed.

On the tenth, the Canadians returned in earnest. The rebels survived several onslaughts until, again, night fell. But the day's battle had cost them dearly in ammunition.

The army bugle sounded again on the eleventh but, for a third day, the Métis held Batoche.

► *May 13*

MR. CARON: I desire to read an important telegram which I received this morning about five o'clock from Major-General Middleton:

Batoche's House, 11th, via Clarke's Crossing, 12th
Have just made a general attack and carried the whole settlement. The rebels in full flight. Sorry to say have not got Riel. While I was reconnoitring this morning, Mr. Astley, one of the prisoners, galloped with a flag of truce and handed me a letter from Riel saying "If you massacre our families I shall massacre the prisoners." I sent answer that if he would put his women and children in one place and let me know where it was, not a shot should be fired on them. I then returned to camp and pushed on my advance parties, who were heavily fired on. I so pressed on until I saw my chance and ordered a general advance. The men responded nobly, drove the enemy out of rifle pits. After rifle pits, forced their way across the plain and seized the houses, and we were masters of the place. Right in the heat of battle, Mr. Astley came back with another missive from Riel as follows: "General, your prompt answer to my note shows that I was right in mentioning to you the cause of humanity. We will gather our families in one place and as soon as it is done we will let you know." On the envelope he had written: "I do not like war and if you do not retreat and refuse an interview, the question remains the same concerning the prisoners." Our loss, I am afraid, heavy; five killed, ten wounded. This is all I know at present. Prisoners all released and safe in my camp. ◄

Again, the military telegrams were not altogether forthcoming. Middleton had angered his men by his timid warfare on the tenth and the eleventh. After the heavy losses during thwarted charges on the first day of battle, Middleton apparently had opted for a slow, one-to-one advance. On the evening of the eleventh, Lt.-Col. A.T.H. Williams decided that if given the opportunity, he would lead a charge. Riel's army had been reduced to 90 men and he knew they were done for.

When the sun rose on May 12, Riel, as the telegraph read in the House had stated, sent Astley the first time. At one o'clock in the afternoon, he suggested to Dumont that they surrender. Dumont refused, hoping that Poundmaker and his warriors would soon arrive. Riel returned to the lines and again recognized the desperate situation of his men. In despair, he sent Astley with the second note. Astley returned with Middleton's condition for a ceasefire: unconditional surrender. It was at that moment that Colonel Williams stood, yelled and waved the Canadians forward. Middleton, realizing that his men had committed themselves, ordered all his troops into the fray. The charge was overwhelming and rebel positions were quickly overrun. Both Riel and Dumont fled. The rebellion was almost over.

▶ *May 15*

MR. CARON: I desire to read to the House a more lengthened report of the battle at Batoche which I have received from the general.

14th May, 1885, from Batoche, N.W.T.
Since my last despatch, I have ascertained some particulars of our victory. Riel and Gabriel Dumont left as soon as they saw us getting well in. Cannot ascertain for certain on which side of the river he is but think must be this side. The extraordinary skill displayed making rifle pits at the exact proper points, and the number of them, is very remarkable. Had we advanced rashly or heedlessly I believe we might have been destroyed.

I reconnoitred to my right front with all my mounted men yesterday morning, with a view to withdrawing as many of their men from my left attack, which was the key of position. On my return to camp, forced on my left and then advanced the whole line with a cheer and a dash worthy of the soldiers of any army. The effect was remarkable. The enemy in front of our left was forced back from pit to pit, and those in the strongest pit, facing east, found them turned and our men behind them.

Then commenced a sauve qui peut and they fled, leaving blankets, coats, hats, boots, trousers and even guns in their pits. I have to regret the death of three officers, as well as two soldiers but they died nobly and well. Nearly the whole of the rebels families were left and are encamped close to the river bank. They were terribly frightened but I have reassured them and protected them. There is a report that Gabriel Dumont is killed but I do not believe it.

This morning, I sent out a letter addressed to Riel as follows: "I am ready to receive you and your council and to protect you until your case has been decided upon by the Dominion Parliament."

I am inclined to think the complete smash of the rebels will have pretty well broken the back of the rebellion. At any rate, it will, I trust, have dispelled the idea that half-breeds and Indians can withstand the attack of resolute whites, properly led, and will tend to remove the unaccountable scare that seems to have entered into the minds of so many in the Northwest, as regards the prowess and powers of fighting of the Indians and breeds.

Fred. Middleton ◄

On May 13, Riel and Dumont parted company, never to see each other again. Riel declined Dumont's offer to hide in the United States. On May 15, while Riel was trying to decide whether he would accept Middleton's latest offer, three Northwest Mounted Police spotted him.

► *May 16*

MR. CARON: Before the orders of the day are called, I wish to read a telegram received from General Middleton:

Clarke's Crossing, 15th
Riel my prisoner.

Frederick Middleton ◄

The 48-day rebellion was over. Gabriel Dumont had escaped to the United States, where he joined a travelling circus as a sharpshooter. Poundmaker surrendered on May 26. Big Bear was apprehended on July 2, 1885, just 18 days before the case of *The Queen versus Louis Riel* began in a Regina courthouse.

4

The Changing
of the Guard

▶▶▶▶▶▶▶▶▶▶▶▶▶▶▶

THE RIEL RESOLUTION
▶▶▶▶▶▶▶▶▶▶▶▶▶▶

IMMEDIATELY **AFTER** THE EXECUTION of Louis Riel, hanged in
Regina on November 16, 1885, for high treason, Macdonald
retired to winter in England. It was there that he learned of the
massive demonstration in Champs de Mars Square, Montreal,
on November 22, where Wilfrid Laurier and 36 other speakers
worked the crowd into a frenzy. On January 11, 1886, Macdonald turned 71. Six weeks later, he was back in Ottawa presiding
over the start of the Fourth (and last) Session of the Fifth
Parliament.

The dreaded resolution came on March 11, 1886. Thirty-two
words, designed to divide and conquer the ruling Conservative
party. Thirty-two words, straight from the heart of Quebec, and
crafted with great care: "That this House feels it its duty to
express its deep regret that the sentence of death passed upon
Louis Riel, convicted of high treason, was allowed to be carried
into execution."

The mover was Auguste-Charles-Phillipe-Robert Landry, the
Conservative member for Montmagny. "Mr. Speaker, on the
16th of November last, Louis Riel was launched into eternity,"
he bellowed. "Let it be recorded as a disgrace to mankind."

Landry, Macdonald, Mackenzie, Blake: they all knew the dangers of this motion. French-Canadians were appalled that a fellow French-Canadian, allegedly insane, would escape the mercy of the Crown and the commutation of his sentence of death.

The sentiments of many Ontario residents were expressed in an edition of the Toronto *Mail*, published 13 days before Riel was executed. "As Britons, we believe the conquest will have to be fought over again, and Lower Canada may depend upon it. There will be no treaty of 1763. The victors will not capitulate next time. The French-Canadian people would lose everything. The wreck of their fortunes and their happiness would be swift, complete and irremediable."

The debate that followed marked a historic transition in the province of Quebec. Hector Langevin, the minister of public works, had, since 1873, replaced George-Etienne Cartier as Macdonald's Quebec lieutenant. Langevin was a Father of Confederation and had been a member of Macdonald's first cabinet in 1867. In the 1885 cabinet decision not to commute Riel's sentence from death to life in prison, Langevin had held steady with his anglophone colleagues, although it would cost him his political future.

"It is always a painful duty to allow a fellow creature to go to the scaffold," pleaded Langevin to a packed House and gallery. "We have been, for our action, insulted and blackened as no men in the world have been. Whether that man had French blood in his veins, or whether he had English or Irish or Scotch blood, the government had only to consider whether he was guilty or not."

Strangely, this debate would have greater consequence for the Liberal party. Their great leader, Edward Blake, now 52, had been discredited when a damaging telegram was read into the record on March 12 by Conservative Nathaniel Wallace, the member for York West. Like Macdonald, Blake had retreated to England during the fall furore.

"There was once a turkey sitting on a fence," Wallace had joked, just before revealing the contents of the telegram. "First, he looked on one side and then on another side. He scratched his ear with his toe and then dropped down on the side on which there is most corn for his party." Wallace then read a telegram in which Blake urged that "unless we gain advantage of this crisis, we are done for." It was a blatant declaration of political opportunism, without any apparent concern for the national interest.

Debate resumed on March 16. For a brief moment, with Blake's response still awaited, the House fell silent; nobody from the government ranks rose. The Speaker glanced around the House. At first, Wilfrid Laurier remained in his seat. The shy member for Quebec East expected more government members to participate in the debate. But then, sensing that the Speaker could not long allow silence without calling for the vote, he rose.

► **WILFRID LAURIER** (Quebec East): Since no one on the other side of the House has the courage to continue this debate, I will do so myself.

Sir, amongst the race to which I belong, the execution of Louis Riel has been universally condemned as being the sacrifice of a life, not to inexorable justice, but to bitter passion and revenge.

The movement has been strangely misconceived. The Tory press of Ontario turned bitterly and savagely upon their French allies. They charged the whole French race that the only motive which led them to take the course they did was simply because Riel was of French origin.

Sir, I denounce this as a vile calumny. I claim this for my fellow countrymen of French origin that there is not to be found anywhere, under heaven a more docile, quiet and law-abiding people. Whatever their faults may be, it is not one of their faults to shield, conceal and abet crime.

I will not admit that blood relations can so far cloud my judgement as to make me mistake wrong or right. But I cheerfully admit and I will plead guilty to that weakness, if weakness it be, that if an injustice be committed against a fellow being, the blow will fall deeper into my heart if it should fall upon one of my kith and kin.

Sir, rebellion is always an evil. It is always an offence against the law of a nation. It is not always a moral crime. What is hateful is not rebellion but the despotism which induces that rebellion. What is hateful are not rebels but the men who, having the enjoyment of power, do not discharge the duties of power. They are the men who, having the power to redress wrongs, refuse to listen to the petitions that are sent to them. They are the men who, when they are asked for a loaf, give a stone.

I appeal to every friend of liberty, to all those who, during twenty-five years past, have felt their hearts thrill whenever a struggle for freedom was going on in any corner of the world. With the Italians, when they delivered their country from the yoke of Austria! With the Americans, in their stupendous struggle for national unity! With the Mexicans, in their successful attempt to resist the foreign domination which the French Emperor sought to impose on them! And when, at last — at last — a section of our countrymen rose in arms to claim rights long denied them, rights that were immediately acknowledged to be just, as soon as they were asked with bullets, are we to have no sympathy with them?

As the execution of the Duke D'Enghien is a stain on the memory of Napoleon; as the execution of Louis XVI is a stain on the records of the French Convention; as the execution of the Admiral Byng is a stain on the English government of the day; as the execution of Mary Stuart is a stain on the memory of Queen Elizabeth, the execution of Riel will be a permanent stain and shame on the present government. ◄

Prime Minister John Macdonald was bedridden, suffering from a serious bout of bronchitis and, conveniently, could not participate in the debate.

Blake rose in the House on March 19. In his autobiography, *Reminiscences*, Sir Richard Cartwright described the atmosphere in the House of Commons during Blake's seven-hour drawling monotone on the Riel resolution. "Glancing around," Cartwright recalled, "I saw that our friends were all, as in duty bound, in solid phalanx in their places, but also, alas, that the majority of them were fast asleep!"

On March 29, to end the factious debate, the government moved "that the question be now put," which would force a vote on Landry's motion. This motion carried 126–73. Then Speaker George Kirkpatrick (Frontenac) called for a division on Landry's motion. It was defeated 146–52. Seventeen French Conservatives voted with Landry; twenty-three English Liberals voted against it. It has been said that never before or since have the members of the House of Commons split so cleanly along linguistic lines.

Unbeknownst then to Macdonald, the political price for the execution of Louis Riel would be enormous. For 17 consecutive federal elections from 1887 to 1958, Quebec spurned the federal Conservative party.

A PROPOS DE RIEN
▶▶▶▶▶▶▶▶▶▶▶▶

DURING THE FOUR YEARS that Wilfrid Laurier was leader of the opposition and John A. Macdonald was prime minister, June 1887 to June 1891, the House of Commons witnessed the best leader-against-leader battles it would ever know. The old Chieftain never lost his ability for public speaking, an ability his enemies said was his only political ability. Laurier was much younger but demonstrated early his prowess in debate. Sadly, the most frequent opportunity for them to face off came over resolutions that pitted French against English, Protestant

against Catholic. As prime minister, Macdonald could have none of that volatile game, although Laurier tried again and again to pin him down.

On the order paper, the bill seemed harmless enough: An Act to amend the Revised Statutes of Canada respecting the Northwest Territories. But its mover, Dalton McCarthy (North Simcoe), had designed his proposal so as to disallow the use of French in the developing territories of northwestern Canada (soon to be Saskatchewan and Alberta). The preamble of the bill read, "Whereas it is expedient in the interest of national unity in the Dominion that there should be a community of language among the people of Canada."

Canada's two best-known prime ministers squared off on February 17, 1890, under the glare of new electric lights.

▶ **WILFRID LAURIER** — Leader of the Opposition (Quebec East): I can find nothing in this bill but the old spirit of domination and intolerance which, in this land, and in other lands, has always characterized the course of pure, unadulterated Toryism. This measure constitutes a declaration of war by the hon. gentleman against the French race. I have here his language which he used no later than the 12th of July last, at Stayner, Ontario, where he said:

> . . . the great danger which overshadowed Canada was the French nationality cry, this bastard nationality, not a nationality that will take us in as we will take them in, but a nationality which begins and ends with the French race; which begins and ends with those who profess the Roman Catholic faith and who now threaten the dismemberment of Canada.

Why, Sir, the days are not five years distant when this "bastard nationality" was unanimous in their support to the Conservative party; when the hon. gentleman might have counted on his fingers the members of that race in this House who did not belong to the Conservative party. A danger to Canada, Sir! I venture to say, judging of the future by the past, that if the French-Canadians were again to unite and give the whole weight of their influence to the party to which the hon. gentleman belongs, not one word more would we hear about this danger to Canada from the French national cry!

I would be inclined to say: "let this measure pass." But this is not the last movement of the hon. gentleman. This is only a preliminary skirmish, soon to be followed by a general onslaught upon the whole French race in Canada. His object is a hand-to-hand conflict with the French race in Canada. There is no mistaking his meaning that his ultimate object is the annihilation of the French race as an individual people in this Dominion. The French-Canadians are to be deprived of their language, not only in the Northwest Territories, but wherever their language exists. If not done by legislation, in future it will be done by force and violence; by bullets and bayonets.

The future of Canada is this: it must be British. I do not share the dreams or the delusions of my fellow countrymen of French origin, who talk to us of forming a French nation on the banks of the St. Lawrence; and I would say to my hon. friend from Simcoe that these dreams ought not to disturb his sleep. Those who share these delusions are very few. They might be counted upon the fingers of one hand and I never knew but one newspaper which ever gave them utterance.

RIGHT HON. SIR JOHN A. MACDONALD — Prime Minister (Kingston): I go a great way with my hon. friend in his remarks concerning the principles of this bill. I have no accord with the desire expressed in some quarters that by any mode whatever there should be an attempt made to oppress the one language or to render it inferior to the other. I believe it would be impossible if it were tried and it would be foolish and wicked if it were possible. The statement that has been made so often that this is a conquered country is *à propos de rien*. There is no paramount race in this country. There is no conquered race in this country. We are all British subjects and those who are not English are none the less British subjects on that account.

The greatest, perhaps, of all the objections to this measure is that it is a futile measure. It will not succeed. It cannot succeed. In order to carry out an oppressive measure we must have a Russian government or we must have a Strafford here! We must put down the language with a strong hand! We must exclude it from schools! We must exclude it from official life! No man in Canada who spoke French must be allowed to take office! The Frenchman must be made a pariah and his language must be made a mark of scorn! That is the only way to carry out the principle or the object of my hon. friend the minister for North Simcoe. . . .

SOME HON. MEMBERS: Hear, hear!

MR. MACDONALD: Did I call my hon. friend the minister from North Simcoe? That is giving him more than equal rights!

His proposal is like the sting of a gnat; a sort of irritation which can be of no use. There is scarcely any French spoken in the Northwest. Unless it be that my hon. friend has a dislike to the language or to the people who use that language, I cannot understand why he has pressed this bill. With the little exception of the slight touch of partisanship in the speech of my hon. friend who spoke last (Mr. Laurier), the speeches of the gentlemen who have honoured the House have been of a kind that I agree with almost everything they say. ◄

After five days of debate, McCarthy's bill went down to defeat, with Macdonald and Laurier again voting together. Their unified condemnation was of incalculable influence and guided the country safely through a number of anti-French measures that would sporadically plague Parliament in the decade to come.

"McCarthy has sown the Dragon's teeth," Macdonald wrote to a friend. "God only knows what the results may be."

Later during that same month, March 1890, the Manitoba government abolished French and denominational schools, thus setting the stage for the six-and-a-half-year battle of the Manitoba School Question, a controversy that would thrust the Conservative party into such turmoil, Laurier would reign as prime minister for an uninterrupted fifteen years.

DEATH OF THE OLD CHIEFTAIN
►►►►►►►►►►►►►►►►►►►

I**T WAS SATURDAY,** May 23, 1891. Although slightly feverish, Macdonald attended a cabinet meeting all day. When he arrived at Earnscliffe, his residence just off Sussex Street, at 6 p.m., he required his wife's assistance to climb the steps. Guests were expected for dinner, and Macdonald insisted that the affair not be cancelled. His guests would later recall that Sir John appeared to be his normal self that evening.

The next day, the pains came in earnest. On May 27, he suffered a stroke and lost sensation in the left side of his body. Two Ottawa specialists examined him on the twenty-eighth, but by then he had recovered the use of his limbs.

At 4 p.m. on May 29, Macdonald suffered another stroke, which left the right side of his body paralysed. He could no longer speak.

In the House of Commons, a message was brought in and discreetly handed to Hector Langevin. He read it and whispered softly to other ministers gathered around him. Then he stood and crossed the floor and told Wilfrid Laurier the tragic news. Langevin returned to his seat and rose.

Speaker Peter White (North Renfrew) interrupted the debate when Langevin rose. "I have the painful duty to announce to the House that the First Minister is in a most critical condition. The medical men do not seem to believe that he can live much longer." The House adjourned immediately.

For seven days he lingered, able to communicate only by squeezing his left hand. Then, at 10:24 p.m., Saturday, June 6, the corps of journalists holding vigil at the front gate of the prime minister's residence recognized his secretary, Joseph Pope, slowly walking down the Earnscliffe pathway.

"Gentlemen, Sir John Macdonald is dead," Pope said. "He died at a quarter past ten."

The body of John A. Macdonald lay at Earnscliffe for two days and then moved to lie in state in the chamber of the Senate. The House of Commons reopened at three o'clock on Monday, June 8.

► **SIR HECTOR LANGEVIN** — Minister of Public Works (Trois-Rivières): Mr. Speaker, our dear old chief, the First Minister of Canada, is no more. After a painful illness of two weeks, death put an end to his earthly career on Saturday evening last. By the death of Sir John A. Macdonald, Canada has lost its greatest statesman, a great patriot, a man of whom any country in the world would be justly proud.

For nearly fifty years he directed the affairs of this country. He was among the Fathers of Confederation the most prominent and distinguished. He put his whole soul into that great undertaking, knowing full well that the confederation of all the British North American provinces would give to our people a country and institutions to be glorious of. He told me more than once how grateful he was to the people of Canada to have allowed him to have consolidated that great work.

Mr. Speaker, I would have wished to continue to speak of our dear departed friend, and spoken to you about his goodness of heart, the witness of which I have been so often, but I feel that I must stop. My heart is full of tears. I cannot proceed further.

WILFRID LAURIER — Leader of the Opposition (Quebec East): Mr. Speaker, I fully realize the emotion which chokes the hon. gentleman. His silence, under the circumstances, is far more eloquent than any human language could be. We on this side of the House who were his opponents, who did not believe in his policy, nor in his methods of government, we take our full share of grief; for the loss which they deplore today is far and away beyond and above the ordinary compass of party range. It is in every respect a great national loss, for he who is no more was, in many respects, Canada's most illustrious son, and in every sense Canada's foremost citizen and statesman.

When, a few days ago in the heat of an angry discussion the news spread in this House, that of a sudden his condition had become alarming, the surging waves of angry discussion were at once hushed, and everyone, friend and foe, realized that this time for a certainty the angel of death had appeared and had crossed the threshold of his home. Yet it is almost impossible to convince the unwilling mind, that it is true, that Sir John Macdonald is no more, that the chair which we now see vacant shall remain forever vacant; that the face so familiar in this Parliament for the last forty years shall be seen no more, and that the voice so well known shall be heard no more.

It may indeed happen, Sir, that when the Canadian people see the ranks thus gradually reduced and thinned of those upon whom they have been in the habit of relying for guidance, that a feeling of apprehension will creep into the hearts lest, perhaps, the institutions of Canada may be imperilled. Before the grave of him who, above all, was the father of confederation, let not grief be barren grief; but let grief be coupled with the resolution, the determination that the work in which Liberals and Conservatives, in which Brown and Macdonald united, shall not perish, but that though United Canada may be deprived of the services of her greatest men, still Canada shall and will live. ◄

After lying in state for two days in the Senate chamber, Macdonald was buried at Cataraqui Cemetery in Kingston on June 11, 1891. His seat on the front benches to the right of the Speaker remained empty, draped in black and covered with flowers, until the end of the First Session of the Seventh Parliament.

Macdonald had served in the House of Commons for 24 years, 19 of those as prime minister. Through his initiatives, British North America had become a confederation of seven provinces and a Northwest Territory, which would soon yield two more. A track of steel and a telegraph line linked the Atlantic and Pacific oceans. The population of Canada had blossomed from 3.5 million in 1867 to 5 million at the time of his death.

During an 1884 Conservative rally to celebrate his fortieth year as a politician, Macdonald had said, "When I look back through my forty years of public life; when I remember how few remain of those who with me entered full of hope, life and the earnestness of youth; when I bear in mind that those who do remain are like myself, feeble old men . . . "

Just then, someone cried out, "No! No! You'll never die, John A."

WOMEN'S SUFFRAGE
▶▶▶▶▶▶▶▶▶▶▶▶▶

THE FIRST ATTEMPT in the House of Commons at conferring the right to vote upon women had been made by Sir John A. Macdonald. "A majority of this House are opposed to female suffrage," Macdonald acknowledged when he introduced his Franchise Bill in 1885. "I had hoped that Canada would have the honour of first placing woman in the position that she is certain, eventually, after centuries of oppression, to obtain. It is merely a question of time all over the civilized world." But before it became law, the prime minister's Franchise Bill was amended to exclude women's suffrage.

The second attempt was made during Sir Mackenzie Bowell's short tenure as prime minister. Bowell was 70 years old when he took office in 1894, an emergency and compromise choice of a Conservative caucus staggered by the deaths of two of its leaders in four years. With the Manitoba School Question threatening the unity of his Conservative caucus, Bowell was undoubtedly none too pleased when, on May 8, 1895, his own backbencher, Nicholas Flood Davin, stood up in the chamber to table a women's suffrage resolution.

Davin was an Irish-born Canadian who had made his home

in the Northwest Territory. The 52-year-old bachelor moved "that in the opinion of the House, the privilege of voting for candidates for membership thereof should be extended to women possessing the qualifications which now entitle men to the electoral franchise." The proposal would not allow women to be candidates, but simply to vote.

► **NICHOLAS FLOOD DAVIN** (Assiniboia West): Mr. Speaker, look at what women have done in politics. We need not go beyond our own gracious Queen. If they can discharge the highest of political duties, how can they be unfit to discharge one of the smallest duties they can be asked to discharge in the political sphere, namely, to say for whom they may vote to be a member of Parliament.

The enfranchisement of women would elevate the tone of politics. Women are quicker in their perceptions than men. To include them among the electorate would quicken the intelligence and perceptiveness of the constituency. If the House shall sanction this proposition, and so justify me in bringing in the bill that shall translate it into law, I believe this Parliament will take a wise step.

JAMES McMULLEN (Wellington North): I would not be at all surprised to find, in the mover of such a motion, a member who had shown his great appreciation of the fair sex by proposing to one of them and linking his fortunes with her. But to find a confirmed bachelor propose such a motion is, I confess, a surprise.

I think, Sir, that it will take away from the real charm and womanliness of women if they were given the franchise and allowed to mix in politics. I can imagine that I might go home some evening and find, instead of my being expected, with tea on the table, nothing was done, because the absorbing question of the hour was politics. I might find a very nice-looking politician sitting in the parlour soliciting a vote. I am afraid that a good many married men might get tired of the situation.

But seriously, if the franchise were given to women, the question would not stop there. The next thing would be that women would wish to be candidates for Parliament, and some of us would be left out in the cold. I am hardly prepared to vote for that.

SEVERIN LACHAPELLE (Hochelaga): Mr. Speaker, to allow women to vote is, without any necessity, to impose on them a new obligation, a new duty, in addition to those which they have already as daughters, wives and mothers. I have too much regard for women — and this is my way to show them my respect — to impose on them a new function, to overburden their weak shoulders, which could not bear such a heavy burden. Perhaps I am putting myself in opposition to history, which says the French people are essentially a most courteous people. I regret, I say, having to record such an opinion, but I think it is the conclusion to which the House should come.

WILLIAM F. MACLEAN (York): If women had their say in politics today, the country would be ruled by emotion rather than reason. Politics are not suited to the physical limitations which surround her sex. Her Majesty Queen Victoria is held up to us as a great queen and one of the leading politicians of Europe, but there are many who think that even her position would have been better filled by a man.

MR. DAVIN: A man like George IV?

GUILLAUME AMYOT (Bellechasse): Mr. Speaker, we all admit that women are the most beautiful part of humanity. They are, so to say, the point of connection between earth and Heaven. They soothe and alleviate social evils. She is made for the house, for the home of which she is an angel. There would be much imprudence to make a voter of her, to entangle her in the acts of shoving and acts of violence which accompany our political contests. Let us leave them their moral purity, their bashfulness, their sweetness, which give them in our minds so much charm. Providence intended that it be so. It ill-becomes the community to change her sex and to degrade her by the exercise of the franchise. You make men of women and you depotize them.◄

On June 5, 1895, the vote was taken, and Nicholas Davin's resolution was defeated 105 to 47. The exclusive club of male legislators still honestly believed what their ancestors had told them — and perhaps also that the earth was flat.

NEST OF TRAITORS
►►►►►►►►►►►►

THE **GOVERNMENT** of Manitoba was adamant: they would not repeal their education legislation. Separate schools were too expensive and the division of resources favoured the smaller Roman Catholic schools. Since the Manitoba law was passed in

1890, three legal battles were fought on the matter, each going to final appeal before the Privy Council in England. The highest courts had confirmed the authority of provincial governments to do away with dual school systems, one for Protestants and another for Roman Catholics.

At first, the federal cabinet tried to negotiate with the Manitoba legislative council. The Manitoba Act provided for an appeal to the Governor General of any grievances with regards to education laws enacted by the Manitoba Legislative Assembly. The Governor General could enact remedial legislation under the advice of the federal cabinet.

In May 1894, a petition signed by no fewer than 31 Roman Catholic bishops landed on the desk of Canada's first Roman Catholic prime minister, John Thompson, urging disallowance of the provincial bill. Thompson told the government of Manitoba to amend its proposal or face remedial federal legislation. The die was cast for a showdown.

In December 1894, Thompson died suddenly while visiting Queen Victoria in England. He was replaced by Mackenzie Bowell. In June of 1895, the Manitoba legislature called the federal bluff and stated it would not obey the federal order. Immediately, the soul-wrenching of Bowell's mixed cabinet, made up mostly of Protestants, raged intense. Three Quebec ministers insisted that remedial legislation be forthcoming immediately. Before long, Auguste Réal Angers, the minister of agriculture, resigned in disgust, exasperated by the prolonged indecision.

The speech from the throne opened the 1896 session of Parliament and promised remedial legislation. That was likely the primary reason for Adolphe Caron's announcement in the House of Commons. But for the ministers concerned, political convenience dictated that Bowell's inability to replace Angers was cited as the primary reason for what transpired on January 7, 1896.

▶ **SIR ADOLPHE CARON** — Postmaster General (Rimouski): Mr. Speaker, I have an important announcement to make to the House. Seven members of the cabinet have tendered their resignations to the prime minister, which were accepted by the Governor General: George Foster, minister of finance; John Haggart, minister of railways and canals; Sir Charles Hibbert Tupper, minister of justice; William Ives, minister of trade and commerce; Arthur Dickey, minister of militia and defence; Walter Montague, minister of agriculture; and John Wood, controller of customs.

Considering the gravity of the situation, I move that when the House adjourns this day, it do stand adjourned until Tuesday the 21st.

GEORGE FOSTER (King's–N.B.): Mr. Speaker, before the House adjourns, I rise to perform a duty which I conceive should be performed at once.

The Liberal-Conservative party ought to be represented by the strongest government possible to be secured from its ranks. We believe that such a government can be formed without delay. This we have repeatedly urged upon the premier with the result that we found ourselves face to face with Parliament having a government with its numbers incomplete and with no assurance that the present premier could satisfactorily complete it. Under these circumstances we thought it our duty to retire, to pave the way for the formation of a government whose premier could command the confidence of all his colleagues and impress the country that it had a government which was united and had power to govern.

SIR RICHARD CARTWRIGHT (Oxford South): Mr. Speaker, it is three and thirty years since I first sat in the Parliament of the then two Canadas. I can recall nothing in the faintest degree parallel with the present conditions of things. Mr. Speaker, no matter what their grounds or their reasons may be, for a cabinet to place a speech in the mouth of His Excellency and then, before the document is dry, to put a pistol to the head of their own colleague, the premier of this country — to place him in the utterly humiliating and degrading position in which they have tried to place him — is utterly unparalleled in the history of any British community. Neither, Sir, is it a less insult to the House. I say it is a fraud on the country. If these seven gentlemen long entertained as is perfectly evident from the statement we have just heard, such sentiments against the leader of the government as have been expressed, each and every one of them have openly and shamefully perpetrated a fraud upon the electorate of the country. ◄

The House then adjourned. The next day, before the Speaker could read the orders of the day, Caron again stood to be recognized. He had no further information for the House, and he again requested an immediate 10-day adjournment. Leader of the opposition Wilfrid Laurier refused. But by now, proper notice had been given to Caron's motion for a 10-day hiatus. On Thursday, January 9, Caron's motion came up — with yet another bombshell. Caron announced that Bowell had tendered his resignation to Governor General the Earl of Aberdeen, but Aberdeen had refused it. Now, Caron asked for a four-day adjournment of the House.

"An adjournment of more than a day is altogether contrary to the spirit of our constitution," wailed Laurier.

Laurier wanted the government to appear in the House every day, to cripple it even further by daily questioning. But Caron's motion carried. Then, on the fourteenth, he again requested a one-day adjournment. This time, he promised the House that a reconstructed cabinet would be announced. On January 15, the crisis ended.

► **MR. CARON:** Mr. Speaker, the prime minister has satisfied himself that the best interests of the country would be served by the return to their former positions in the cabinet of those who deemed it their duty to retire. Since the receipt of the resignations referred to, the objections put forward by the ministers who resigned have been removed by the acceptance of a seat in the cabinet by the Hon. Alphonse Desjardins, a gentleman well known and esteemed in the province of Quebec for his ability and integrity of character, and by the acceptance to the ministry of Sir Charles Tupper, Baronet. The ministers who resigned have deemed it consistent with duty to their country to resume the positions they held in the government.

MR. LAURIER: So, at last, Mr. Speaker, after these long days of waiting, after the public business has been blocked for almost two weeks, after the House has been subjected to the ignominy of dancing attendance upon the pleasure of weak and vacillating men. At last the comedy is at an end. The stray sheep have gone back to the fold. The bolters have eaten their words and they are expected to sit again under the man who just a week ago yesterday, they declared was too small to be their leader. Everybody might have expected it. These ministerial crises are becoming ludicrously monotonous in their regularity and in their sameness. A few days out in the cold and they return to the fold. A general kissing and embracing, an admission and confession of guilt, pardon from all sides, and everything serene and lovely on the surface; though, I presume, still underneath there is a great deal of kicking and swearing and cursing and vilifying each other.

Sir, if the country has been impressed in any way, it has been impressed with the conviction which now prevails that the government is composed of a brand of plotters and schemers and conspirators. Sir, today, have we a complete government? No, Sir, we have still the rump of a government.

SIR RICHARD CARTWRIGHT: Mr. Speaker, let us consider for a moment what this whole farce means. This whole business has been transacted for the purpose, and for no other purpose, than to make room for my ancient acquaintance, Sir Charles Tupper, Baronet of the United Kingdom. Sir, is it impossible that ever such a crew as I see yonder could dream of returning except on a most distinct understanding, whether written or verbal, that within a very short space of time Sir Mackenzie Bowell must make way for Sir Charles Tupper.

Sir, I am sorry to say for Sir Mackenzie Bowell, he cannot expect the same measure of our sympathy and respect when he sinks to play the part of a warming-pan to one of the most corrupt politicians our country has ever known. Sir Charles Tupper, Bart., is a very ancient acquaintance of mine. The fame of Sir Charles Tupper, if not precisely well known in all the churches, is well known in all the provinces of this Dominion. Nova Scotia has produced so many eminent men, but which has also been the dry-nurse, aye, and the wet-nurse too, of the most highly developed type of Tory boodlers this country has ever known.

It is in the recollection of some hon. gentlemen here that the premier, in the hearing of many gentlemen around me, described himself not many days ago, on the floor of the House, as having been living in a nest of traitors. In his place in the Senate chamber, the premier declared that the conduct of his colleagues to him had been unparalleled in British history. He feared they were a set of ruffians who had no reverence for grey hairs.

The minister of finance with exceedingly little circumlocution, declared that the premier of Canada was an old fool, and an obstinate one at that.

GEORGE FOSTER — Minister of Finance (King's, N.B.): *Ipsissima verba*.

MR. CARTWRIGHT: Well. I think that is an accurate if not a literal translation.

It is my happy privilege to be able to afford a side light as to how they strike our neighbours, the citizens of the great American Republic. As it happened very recently, four of these hon. gentlemen were travelling either in the United States or in the immediate vicinity of the United States. They were, as I am informed, the hon. minister of trade and commerce, the hon. minister of agriculture, the hon. minister of finance and hon. minister of railways. They were travelling in an ordinary Pullman car like common mortals such as you and me. Mr. Speaker, a friend of mine pointed them out to an American gentleman travelling with him as distinguished Canadian luminaries. He regarded them long and carefully, and when asked his opinion of them delivered it in these few words: "Stranger, if them four fellers are Privy Councillors and advisers of Her Majesty Queen Victoria, then, stranger, I never said it before and I never thought to say it at all, but I so say now and say it from the very bottom of my heart, God Save the Queen." ◄

Although the dust soon settled within the halls of Parliament, the electorate would not forget the charade. Charles Tupper, Sr., was back, as secretary of state no less, but he would first be required to secure a seat in the House. All the while, the Manitoba School Question remained unresolved and continued to undermine the public's confidence in the Conservative party.

Assuming power after Bowell's resignation in late April, Sir Charles Tupper presided over the Canadian government for barely more than two months, the shortest term of any Canadian prime minister. After 18 consecutive years in office, the Conservatives went down to defeat in the June 23, 1896, federal election. The Liberal party, under the leadership of Wilfrid Laurier, would reign over the federal government for fifteen unbroken years.

5

New Horizons

▶▶▶▶▶▶▶▶▶▶▶▶▶▶▶▶▶▶▶

ALBERTA AND SASKATCHEWAN IN; SIFTON OUT
▶▶▶▶▶▶▶▶▶▶▶▶▶▶▶▶▶▶▶▶▶▶▶▶▶▶▶▶▶▶▶▶▶▶▶

SINCE 1876, THE PRESENT PROVINCES of Alberta and Saskatchewan had been organized as a single territory, under the
name once held by the province of Manitoba: the Northwest
Territory. Both regions had been theatres of insurrection. As
Manitoba had seen the Red River Métis take up arms in 1870,
so had the new Northwest, in 1885. Again, Louis Riel had raised
his people to rebel. Again, he had been defeated. Although he
had paid for his insurgency with his life, the uprising had
abruptly turned eastern Canada's attention to the shores of the
Saskatchewan River.

In 1905, it had been 35 years since Canada had admitted
Manitoba into Confederation. The young nation now included
seven provinces. The new Northwest Territory was complete
with a premier, but the local legislature was limited to scant
jurisdictions granted by the federal government. By the early
1900s, the population of the territory was mushrooming. The
1901 census showed 165,555 settlers upon the territory. By
1904, the population had reached 417,956; only Ontario, Quebec and Nova Scotia had more citizens. With immigration rates
as high as they were, some were predicting that this number
would again double in the next few years.

By the turn of the century, territorial Conservative premier
Frederick Haultain began to correspond with federal officials

on the subject of provincial autonomy. It was not long before the matter became the biggest political issue of the Northwest.

In spite of the recent controversy over the Manitoba School Question, educational considerations were strangely absent from preliminary autonomy discussions between the Northwest Territories and the government of Canada. According to an open letter written to Prime Minister Laurier by Premier Haultain as late as March 12, 1905: "Educational clauses [were] not laid before my colleague or myself until 12 o'clock on the day the bills received first reading."

Negotiations began in earnest between Laurier and Haultain in the first days of January 1905. When Parliament met on January 12, the speech from the throne announced the government's intention to table an autonomy bill. The public was at first treated to scant details, although it was announced on January 19 that the territory would be divided into two territories and that the border would run north and south.

When Prime Minister Sir Wilfrid Laurier introduced the bills to provide for the establishment of the provinces of Saskatchewan and Alberta on February 21, 1905, he tabled documents that had not been discussed or negotiated at the cabinet table. Nor had the leader of the opposition, Robert Borden, been given a copy, until minutes before Laurier rose to speak in the House.

Laurier's particular proposal with regards to education came as a disappointment to his minister of the interior, Clifford Sifton. The subject matter of the bill lay squarely within Sifton's ministerial and regional responsibilities and yet, incredibly, he also had not seen a copy of the bill until it was tabled in the House. Moreover, Sifton was a Manitoba MP and had, while a member of the provincial cabinet in 1896, fought hard to abolish the unconditional right to separate schools. His accession to the federal Liberal cabinet in 1896 had been part of Laurier's compromise package settling the Manitoba–Canada school controversy. Sifton's interest in the matter could not have been accidentally overlooked.

Sifton had fallen very ill in January of 1905. The media had speculated that his absence had been a primary reason for the initial delays in securing an agreement between the territorial and Dominion officials on provincial autonomy. While convalescing in Indiana, he had cabled Laurier one month before the bill was tabled to say, "You do not say anything about the schools question. I assume that you have not as yet discovered any serious difficulty with it." He received a reply on the day before first reading that the "bill will be introduced." Ominously, one of Haultain's ministers had told a reporter from the Toronto *Globe*: "We have no school question on our hands and do not expect any."

Laurier's bill, at first reading, extended generous separate school rights to the residents of the proposed provinces of Alberta and Saskatchewan. Although all other matters paled in comparison to the political crisis in Ottawa, Laurier did offer to the House the reasons for the new inductees into the Canadian confederation. Somewhere in his defensive speech given in the House of Commons on February 21, he found room to remark: "We live by the side of a nation whose example I would not take in everything, in whose schools for fear that Christian dogmas in which all do not believe might be taught. When I compare these two countries, when I observe in this country of ours a total absence of lynchings and an almost total absence of divorces and murders, I thank heaven that we are living in a country where the young children of the land are taught Christian morals and dogmas."

Back in Indiana, Sifton was stunned. According to most historians, this heavy-handedness was not typical of Laurier. The Quebec prime minister was under tremendous pressure from religious and political groups in his home province to accommodate Catholic and French interests as new territories were opened in Canada's western territories. In a book entitled *Laurier et son temps*, published soon after the controversy by Liberal Senator Laurent-Olivier David of Montreal, a friend of the prime minister, the author theorized that Laurier feared civil war if he bungled the Alberta/Saskatchewan bill. Too many political controversies had arisen in Canada in recent years pitting English against French and Protestant against Catholic. Apparently, just before caving in to the enormous pressure to allow the two new provinces to set their own educational programs, Laurier offered to resign if the bill could pass as presented on first reading.

On that February day in the Commons, the opposition tore through Laurier on the conspicuous absence of Sifton. They would soon find out the extent to which Laurier had acted singlehandedly. Ten days later, on March 1, 1905, Laurier had an announcement to make, an announcement that would generate many more questions from a Conservative opposition that had not experienced government for nine years.

▶ **RIGHT HON. SIR WILFRID LAURIER** — Prime Minister (Quebec East): I have to inform the House that my colleague, the hon. Mr. Sifton, has resigned his position in the government, and as minister of the interior. Mr. Sifton finds himself unable to agree with the terms of the bill which has lately been introduced for the admission into the Dominion of the provinces of Alberta and Saskatchewan, his disagreement being confined altogether to the educational clause. After a conference with him, the following correspondence has been exchanged:

Ottawa, February 27, 1905
Dear Sir Wilfrid:
It is impossible for me to continue in office under present circumstances, and that it is better for all concerned that I should act at once. I therefore beg to tender my resignation as member of the government. I trust that the unhappy necessity which has arisen will not in the least impair the friendship with which you have been kind enough to honour me.
Believe me, yours most faithfully, Clifford Sifton

To this I answered yesterday in the following terms:

Ottawa, February 28, 1905
My dear Sifton:
I received yesterday your letter. There is no alternative for me but to accept it. After our conversation of the other day, I had left you with the impression that the differences between us were more of words than of substance, and until I received your letter, I had cherished the hope that it would be possible ere this to find a comparatively easy solution. Whilst

I feel more regret than I can express at this termination of our official relations, let me assure you that should our old friendship be ever impaired, the fault will not be mine.

Your very sincerely, Wilfrid Laurier ◀

All for naught. Laurier soon accepted the persistent demands from the opposition and members of his own party and backed down from his first reading proposal to set a dual educational system for the new provinces. On March 22, 1905, a peculiar incident occurred when Laurier rose slowly and with his head down. Borden interpreted this as meaning that Laurier did not intend to speak to second reading of the amended bill, and rose to be recognized by the Speaker. Laurier raised his head, saw the leader of the opposition standing and asked Borden for the "privilege of a few remarks." Borden hesitated and then sat down.

▶ **MR. LAURIER:** I am glad that this debate is starting in such an auspicious manner and that both sides are apparently in very good humour and in a very good frame of mind for the discussion. The constitution of Canada has been and is a compromise between different elements in order to produce a great result. It is a compromise in order to unite heterogeneous elements. There are differences of powers, there are exceptions, but all this diversity is intended to promote unity.

We have done pretty well so far in the development of our national institutions. But we have not yet reached the maximum. We have not yet reached the end. We may have a great deal still to do and I hold that we ought always to be ready for the task. I am sure that it will not be too much to say that it will not injure anyone; that it will not do any harm, but on the contrary, will do much good if, whenever we are called upon to apply the principles of the constitution, we apply them, not in any carping sense, but in a broad and generous spirit. ◀

Borden then called for complete provincial autonomy in matters of education. Sifton was heard from on March 24. "Ecclesiasticism in schools always produces inefficiency," he concluded in the House, adding that he would support Laurier's amended bill. On May 3, Borden's amendment was defeated 140–59, and second reading of the bill was passed by the same margin.

Borden and his Conservatives voted against the bill. It may well have been for technical reasons, standing, as he told the

House, "upon the rock of the Constitution," as Borden insisted that the bill be recommitted to study by committee of the whole. In the end, Conservative members registered their votes against the entry of Saskatchewan and Alberta into the Canadian partnership under the conditions of Laurier's bill. It was a damaging mistake. In the 1908 election, Saskatchewan returned nine Liberal candidates out of 10; Alberta returned four of seven.

Laurier had accepted compromise on the educational aspects of the bill and thus, on this politically explosive issue, had once again escaped unscathed.

CONSCRIPTION
▶▶▶▶▶▶▶▶

BY **1917,** the landscape of Canadian politics had changed forever. Sir Wilfrid Laurier, now 78 years old, sat in opposition, having relinquished the prime ministership in a decisive 1911 electoral defeat to Conservative Robert Borden. Since August 1914, Canada had been engaged in world war against Germany. In 1916, the two elder statesmen of Canada agreed to give the Twelfth Parliament an unprecedented Seventh Session, to expire in October 1917. This extension was agreed upon to spare the mostly rural population, depleted of many of its young men, from the inconveniences of a federal election.

On February 3, 1916, a terrible fire destroyed the House of

Commons, killing a member and claiming six other victims. The assembly was moved into temporary quarters in the Victoria Museum.

On May 25, 1917, Prime Minister Robert Borden welcomed the leader of the opposition to his residence at 201 Wurtemberg Street. Borden was fresh from an overseas trip where he had sat in the British War cabinet and experienced the horrors of warfare firsthand, having visited hospitals and trenches. For the prime minister, the requirements of the military effort were paramount, even over domestic political considerations, his own or that of his five-year-old Conservative government. By now, with the Allied forces still unable to penetrate German lines, and with Canadian voluntary enlistment falling from 30,000 a month at the beginning of 1916 to 6,000 by year's end, Borden was convinced that compulsory military service was necessary. Conscription was on Borden's mind, and he told Laurier so. Therefore, why not form a coalition government, with a cabinet formed equally of Liberals and Conservatives, and suspend elections until victory overseas was assured. Again, Borden argued, the country, and in particular the Canadian military command, could not and should not be subjected to the disruption of a federal election.

Liberal leader Laurier thought differently, well aware of the aversion to conscription his fellow Quebecers harboured, due primarily to Canada's continued submission to England in matters of foreign policy.

For 11 days, the two adversaries negotiated. Borden increased his offer, suggesting that an election be held to confirm the coalition government before enforcing a conscription law. He later went further, offering Laurier the power to appoint the Liberal members to the coalition cabinet and veto any of Borden's nominees! But Laurier said no, he could not join a pro-conscription government.

Four days after Laurier's final refusal, Borden tabled his conscription bill in the House of Commons. Arthur Meighen, solicitor general, had already secretly drafted a military service bill, ready in case negotiations with Laurier broke down. On June 11, 1917, Prime Minister Sir Robert Borden moved for leave to introduce

Bill 75, a bill that would put more than a million Canadian men between the ages of 20 and 45 into uniform.

▶ **RIGHT HON. ROBERT BORDEN** — Prime Minister (Halifax): Mr. Speaker, this enactment is based upon a principle which is as old as the principle of self-government. To the state, each citizen owes a duty of service, and the highest duty of all is the obligation to assist in defending the rights, the institutions and the liberties of his country. There never has been, and there never will be, an occasion when that duty could be more manifest, more urgent, or more imperative than at the present time.

Will any honourable gentleman present deny that there is an emergency within the meaning of this statute? In the midst of the most terrific struggle ever known to history no one will seriously doubt the answer. There is more than an emergency; there is a cataclysm; the greatest emergency, the greatest peril ever known, the greatest, I believe, that will ever be known in the history of this Dominion.

I cannot shrink, and I will not shrink, from the determination to support and sustain the Canadian troops now at the front. God speed the day when the gallant men who are protecting and defending us will return to the land they love so well. Only those who have seen them at the front can realize how much they do love this dear land of Canada. They have seen their friends and comrades discoloured and gasping from poison gas at Ypres. They have known what it means to have regiments decimated, to see comrades and brothers struck down. They have held on grimly in the trenches in the Ypres salient and elsewhere against overwhelming numbers and under devastating power of the enemy's artillery when we lacked guns and munitions. They have climbed the heights of the Vimy Ridge and driven the Germans far beyond it. They have fought and died that Canada might live and that the horrors and desolations of war might never be known within our borders. They went forth splendid in their youth and confidence who not once or twice but fifty times have gone over the parapet to seek their rendezvous with death. Let us prove ourselves worthy to call them comrades. Some may have made the supreme sacrifice for Canada even as we speak. Let us summon in thought those brave comrades, firm of heart and strong of purpose, those who have fought, yes and those who shall fight no more, let us summon them in the spirit to our deliberations, let us speak and determine as if they were in our midst. ◄

The bill was then read a first time. Laurier, who had received an advance copy of the bill, declined to comment until a week later, when he stood before a House no longer divided upon party lines. Laurier spoke as though all his Liberal members were united behind him. Many were not.

► **RIGHT HONOURABLE SIR WILFRID LAURIER** — Leader of the Opposition (Quebec East): Mr. Speaker, it has been asked why the labouring class should be opposed to conscription. It has been asked if they were less patriotic. There are no classes of the community upon which the sacrifices, which are involved in war, fall so heavily as upon the labouring classes. If he loses his limbs, or is crippled in any way, the wealthy man comes to a home in which he will find every comfort. But the poor man has to go to a home where he cannot have comforts, since because of his physical infirmity, he can no longer earn his living. It is no wonder that among these classes there should be opposition to the scheme, not because they are less patriotic, but because they feel that if they are to be conscripted, and called upon to pay that tribute with the rest of the community, at least certain things should be done which would somewhat equalize matters. They ask that if they are to be called upon to give their blood, the wealthy class should, at least, give their wealth in support of the cause.

They have asked something more. They have asked that this Parliament should not pass this law until it has had the advantage of being thoroughly debated before the people, and that the people should have the opportunity to express their opinion upon it. Which is the course most conducive to success in the war: compulsion with irritation and bitterness and a sense of intolerance and injustice, or, consultation with consequent union and universal satisfaction all round? This is the cause for which I constitute myself the humble apostle before the Canadian Parliament at this moment.

Mr. Speaker, the English-speaking portion of the community contributed 280,000 men. The number of French-Canadians enlisted was given at 14,000. Is it surprising that there has been so little enlistment in Quebec? If Quebec had been properly appealed to, for my part I believe the people would have responded on an equal footing with the other provinces. Men are composed of flesh and blood, and if my honourable friend had put at the head of recruiting in Quebec a man of their flesh and blood the results would have been different.

What I propose is that we should have a referendum and a consultation of the people upon this question. If we are to have peace, if there is to be unity, we must meet the wishes of the labouring classes, who have asked for this privilege. When the consultation with the people has been had, when the verdict has been pronounced, I pledge my word, my reputation, that to the verdict, such as it is, every man will submit. And I claim to speak at least so far as is concerned the province from which I come. ◄

Thus began six weeks of intense debate. Facts and figures were tossed across the floor of the House as members staked their claim on a side of compulsory military service.

In the Commons, the die was cast. On July 24, Bill 75 received third reading, 102 votes to 44, and was signed by Governor General the Duke of Devonshire on August 28.

In January 1918, enlistment began in earnest, supported by a vast bureaucracy. The legislation defined 10 classes of male citizens, separated by age and occupation, and established Exemption Courts, a Military Service Council, a Board of Selection, Medical Boards and registrars. Borden's bill contained so many loopholes that 95 per cent of conscripts applied for certificates of exemption. Fully 124,588 men were eventually conscripted, but only 24,132 saw battle before German guns were silenced at 11 a.m. on November 11, 1918.

The conscription debate had wreaked havoc with party unity. In the House, five Conservatives voted with the Liberals in opposition. Twenty-two Liberals voted in favour of Borden's bill. Riots broke out in Montreal, and the house of the owner of the pro-conscription newspaper the Montreal *Star* was dynamited.

In the immediate aftermath of Borden's failed attempt to enlist Laurier into a coalition war government, his political advisers quietly began talking to other prominent Liberals. A thorough Canada-wide quest for coalition candidates was conducted in the fall of 1918 by none other than former Liberal cabinet minister Sir Clifford Sifton. Slowly, Liberals from across Canada began forwarding their résumés to Borden.

On October 11, 1918, Borden dissolved his Conservative cabinet and formed a Union cabinet, with 12 Conservative and nine Liberal members. For the first time in Canadian history, not one French-Canadian held a cabinet seat. Borden proposed another extension of Parliament and met with the immediate refusal of 66 Liberal members. The usefulness of the Twelfth Parliament had run out. As much as he had tried to avoid it, Borden would have to go to the people in the midst of a terrible war. Writs were issued, and Ottawa was abandoned by federal politicians for a national election battle with a single issue: conscription.

When the election results were tabulated on December 17, 1917, the Union Government had won 153 seats, the Liberals 82. Most striking was the polarization of votes. Only three Union party candidates were elected in Quebec as the Liberal party took 62 of the 65 seats in the province. In Ontario, the Union party took 74 of the 82 ridings.

Laurier had little to look forward to at the opening of the First Session of the Thirteenth Parliament. Many of his former colleagues sat across the floor of the House, some occupying cabinet benches. A frightening and unprecedented linguistic split had entrenched itself in the composition of Parliament.

THE DEATH OF A PRIME MINISTER
▶▶▶▶▶▶▶▶▶▶▶▶▶▶▶▶▶▶▶▶▶

L**AURIER'S SPIRITS** were on the upswing throughout the winter of 1918. The German army had been beaten and the war had ended in November. The successful reconstruction of the Liberal party was now a distinct possibility. Labour troubles were very much in the forefront of postwar politics, and Laurier saw his party, not the Union or the Conservatives, as holding the key to a labour–industry political alliance. William Lyon Mackenzie King, a former Liberal member of Parliament and Laurier's minister of labour in 1909, had just published a widely acclaimed book entitled *Industry and Humanity*. Combined with the experience and skill of William S. Fielding, Laurier felt that he could soon secure the return of the renegade Union party Liberals, and a suitable change in leadership, be it King or Fielding.

But fate decided otherwise. On Saturday, February 15, Laurier suffered the first of three strokes. He had attended a Canadian Club function at the Château Laurier hotel and then retreated to his office on the Hill, where he momentarily lost consciousness. Confused, Laurier struggled outside. He flagged a streetcar and rode home. He did not mention the faint to his wife, Zoë.

The next morning, while dressing for mass, he was hit by another, much more severe attack. He regained consciousness in the early evening. A priest was summoned and last rites were administered. "I'm not as sick as you think," he protested to his wife just before suffering a third and fatal stroke. He could but whisper "C'est fini." Forty-eight hours later, on the day before the beginning of the Second Session of the Thirteenth Parliament, Canada's seventh prime minister died.

Laurier's 15-year unbroken tenure as prime minister, from 1896 through 1911, has never been equalled. He had also been leader of the official opposition for an equal period. And since Confederation, no person has held the leadership of a Canadian political party for so long. Only his successor, William Lyon Mackenzie King, would come close, with 28 years of service. Nor has any person ever been a member of the House of Commons for 45 years, 42 of those as the hon. member for Quebec East. In an era when it was lawful and customary for party leaders to seek election in two ridings to increase their chances of election, Laurier ran in an unprecedented 18 federal elections.

Prime Minister Borden was not in the House when it reconvened on February 20. He was in England participating in postwar peace talks. Acting Prime Minister Thomas White secured the unanimous consent of the House for a state funeral. For two days, Laurier's body lay in state in the temporary House, the Victoria Museum. His desk was draped in black. On February 25, a tribute was made by Rudolphe Lemieux, a member of Laurier's cabinet from 1906 to 1911. His eulogy ranks among the most inspiring remarks recorded in Hansard.

► **RUDOLPHE LEMIEUX** (Maisonneuve-Gaspé): Mr. Speaker, the shadow of death has stalked through this chamber. A chair stands vacant.

As we gaze upon the flowers strewn about us which, by the morrow, will have withered away, more deeply than ever do we understand the baffling brevity of this life's span, the specious vanity of each and every thing. Sir Wilfrid Laurier is no more.

The last survivor of a great generation. He whose inspiring stature, whose eagle eye and whose white plume recalled those noblemen of the eighteenth century, such as we meet them still in medallions of olden times, is sleeping his last sleep.

Death is a law and not a punishment. No one better understood this profound truth than the eminent statesman whose loss we mourn. Without bitterness, the old gladiator saw himself disarmed as he was about to descend once more into the arena. His spirit passed gently, serenely, as though amidst the darkening shadows of life's falling night the faith of his forefathers had already revealed the gleam of dawn, presage of eternal day.

It does the heart good to recall that throughout his entire career he was ever faithful to his origin and to the finest traditions of his race. He was wont to say, "I love France who gave us birth. I love England who gave us liberty. But the first place in my heart belongs to Canada, my country, my native land." This striking formula was, if I may speak thus, the ideal, the polar star which guided his public life. First and foremost, Laurier was a Canadian. To his French inheritance, he owed his golden tongue, his keen intellectual vision, the boldness and the grandeur of his conceptions. To his contact with the great English school, the school of Burke, Fox, Pitt, O'Connell, Gladstone, he owed his deep practical knowledge of British institutions.

His dream was to unite the two races on the only rational basis: equality of rights, mutual respect and tolerance. He loved this country especially for its ethnic duality which showed him the children of the two greatest races of Europe, henceforth fellow wayfarers towards a common destiny in the boundless spaces of the New World.

Farewell. Close to your resting place, amid maples and poplars, adorned by the coming spring with luxuriant foliage. The field in which you lie, whose tender embrace you received, will be light to you. For it is part of that native land whose history is three centuries old and whose motherly womb will some day cover our meanness with its vastness and shroud our nothingness with its perennity. Adieu!

THE WINNIPEG STRIKE
►►►►►►►►►►►►►►

AT ELEVEN O'CLOCK on May 15, 1919, 30,000 striking workers paralysed the city of Winnipeg. Within days, most services and businesses were shut down as newspaper printers, telegraph operators and postal employees joined the movement. With bands of strikers wandering the streets, the only businesses that dared to operate were those granted special permits by the strike action committee.

At issue was the right to collective bargaining, that final ratification powers of employment contracts be given to unions. However, within the Winnipeg labour movement were those who promoted Bolshevism. Methodist minister William Ivens, editor of the *Western Labour News*, was particularly outspoken. "All you have to do is walk into any industry, tell the owner you are going to take it over and it is done," he urged the Winnipeg strikers. "A new Soviet government is being established."

Eastern observers were quick to discredit the entire movement. In the words of the *Canadian Annual Review*, it was a "deliberate effort by an extremist element in the labour ranks to capture the government of Winnipeg by means of a general strike."

But the concern behind the action of most Winnipeg strikers was not political. Membership in trade unions had tripled in Canada since 1915. The number of labour disruptions grew from 62 in 1915 to 332 in 1919. Insensitive employers fanned the flames of discontent by keeping postwar wages at war levels. In Winnipeg, sporadic demonstrations had already occurred during the previous winter.

Senator Gideon Robertson, Borden's minister of labour, rushed to Winnipeg. The chosen federal strategy was outrage and heavy-handedness. Striking postal workers were ordered to resume work or face dismissal. The provincial government also ordered its employees back to work. On May 27, Borden rose in the House to offer an unequivocal statement on his government's position.

► **RIGHT HON. ROBERT BORDEN** — Prime Minister (King's, Nova Scotia): In this country as well as in other countries the stress and strain of war have made the adjustment of difficulties between employers and employed more difficult. I do not think there is one among us who will not agree that the people are not quite the same, so far as mental poise and balance are concerned, as they were before the war.

It has been alleged in some quarters that as regards the strike at Winnipeg, the government has taken sides. The government has taken no sides in that dispute. If the needs of the people are to be regarded we cannot have in this country a complete dislocation of public services founded upon such reasons as have been put forward by the postal employees of Winnipeg.

The government is in an entirely different situation from a private employer. Especially so in two respects. In the first place, the duties for which public servants are employed have a direct relation to the maintenance of law and order. But in addition to that, it does not employ these people for any purpose of private gain or private interest. It is acting merely as the representative of the people as a whole, under the mandate, and only so long as it has the mandate of the majority of the people's representatives in Parliament.

In appropriate cases, the public servants of the country might ask for and obtain a sort of appeal against the government by arbitration or some other method; but always subject to final approval by Parliament.

In dealing with the situation in Winnipeg, we are absolutely determined that law and order should be maintained. Members of the civil service cannot be permitted to disregard their public duties and to dislocate the public service under the conditions which have arisen in Winnipeg. On the one hand, the government directs them to discharge a public duty, a duty to the whole of the people of this country. On the other hand, another authority directs them to disregard that duty. They must make their choice as to whether they will serve the public as a whole or whether, by disregarding that duty, they will abandon once and for all the public service. ◄

It was a turning point. Bolstered by the decisive federal support (not to mention the presence of 3,000 troops in barracks in Winnipeg) Mayor Charles Gray secured a city council resolution that mirrored the federal public service ultimatum — municipal employees must return to work or face dismissal. Then Gray proclaimed all parades illegal. Royal North-West Mounted Police appeared on the streets. Wildcat sympathy strikes broke out across the country but to little avail. Faced with unemployment, Winnipeg workers began drifting back to work. Then, suddenly, on Tuesday, June 17, the Mounted Police arrested the strike leaders. Winnipeg erupted in violence.

On June 23, 1919, the president of the Privy Council rose in the House to offer a painful account of the bloody riot.

► **NEWTON ROWELL** — President of the Privy Council (Durham): Mr. Speaker, on Friday last, a meeting of strikers sent word to the minister of labour (Mr. Robertson) that the minister should address them, on pain of violence if he refused. The minister of labour sent word to the strikers that he would address them. That, however, apparently was not satisfactory to them and the committee requested a meeting on Saturday morning which was duly held, and at which the minister of labour was present. The Mayor insisted that under no conditions would the proclamation against parades be lifted. The strikers — at least a group of them — insisted that the parade should go on. The Mayor went to the headquarters of the Mounted Police and asked for their cooperation in preserving law and order. That was the joint request of the Mayor and the Attorney General of the province.

The Mounted Police were thereupon called out and moved down Main Street, endeavouring to disperse the crowd. There was evidence of violence almost at once — so much so that the Mayor read the Riot Act and then proceeded to militia headquarters and asked that the militia be called out.

As I say, there were acts of violence. A street car was seriously broken up. Bricks, stones and other missiles were thrown at the Mounted Police and shots were fired from the mob. The condition was such that the officer in command of the police felt it absolutely necessary, as a matter of self-defence, that the police should fire. This they did. The latest report is that the total number of casualties was thirty-four of which sixteen were in the Mounted Police. Of the men in the crowd who suffered casualties, one was killed.

The militia came immediately to the assistance of the Mounted Police and the mob was dispersed in the course of half an hour. Since that time, the city has been quiet. Up to 7:30 p.m. last evening some 80 arrests have been made.

Everyone must regret that life has been lost on this occasion. Everyone must regret that serious casualties have been sustained. But I am sure that members of this House and the sane and thoughtful people of the country will agree that law and order in Canada must be maintained. ◀

On June 26, the strike was officially called off. A royal commission of inquiry struck by the provincial government identified the causes of the strike: long hours, low wages, growing awareness by the working class of the inequalities of modern society, and the reluctance of employers to accept collective bargaining.

In the aftermath of the Winnipeg strike, two political events occurred that would alter the course of Canadian federal politics. Borden's minister of agriculture, Thomas Crerar (Marquette, Manitoba), resigned, ostensibly because Borden refused to lower tariffs, a move that, Crerar argued, was necessary to reduce the price of farm equipment. Crerar formed the Progressive party, which enjoyed unprecedented success in the 1921 election, with 65 members elected to the 235-member House, compared to the Conservatives' 50. The two-party monopoly of Canadian federal politics was broken forever. The new political force would play a major role in shaping events in the House of Commons for the next seven years.

Then, on August 7, 1919, the minister of labour under Wilfrid Laurier in 1909, William Lyon Mackenzie King, was elected leader of the Liberal party of Canada. King had written in 1918: "Industry exists for the sake of humanity, not humanity for the sake of industry." Words like these and memories of the violent resolution of the Winnipeg strike did much to endear King to Canadian workers during the 1921 federal election campaign, which delivered 116 Liberal members and a majority government.

6

At the Political Crossroads
▶▶▶▶▶▶▶▶▶▶▶▶▶▶▶

THE CUSTOMS SCANDAL
▶▶▶▶▶▶▶▶▶▶▶▶▶▶▶

THE **SPEECH FROM** THE THRONE had been read and a cabinet sworn in to begin the Fifteenth Parliament. William Lyon Mackenzie King's by-election in Prince Albert had been set for February 15 and for now, at least, the prospects of the minority Liberal government surviving the session were alive. The prime minister was busy campaigning in Prince Albert, unaware that political disaster was about to hit.

His nightmare began just before midnight, February 2, 1926. Justice Minister Ernest Lapointe wanted a quick vote on the throne speech so the House might recess for six weeks, time for King to get re-elected. The Liberal strategy kicked into high gear when a motion by Arthur Meighen to amend the government's proposed reply to the speech was defeated 125–115. Conservative Donald Sutherland (Oxford North) moved the adjournment of the debate on the address, a motion that would thwart Lapointe's plans for a six-week parliamentary recess. The Conservative tactic failed 124–115. When Speaker Rudolphe Lemieux announced the division, there was a short sputter of protest from Sutherland. Then the Conservative opposition played their trump. Harry Stevens rose. "His tale," wrote

Stevens' biographer Richard Wilbur, "made the Pacific Scandal of Sir John Macdonald's day seem like the mildest bit of impropriety."

► **HENRY HERBERT STEVENS** (Vancouver Centre): Mr. Speaker, a very grave and serious condition of affairs exists in this country in connection with this government. Already nine filing cabinets filled with records containing damaging evidence have been removed from the custody and the care of the government, taken away down to the home of an ex-minister and there destroyed. I charge this government with knowledge for a year — members of the government including the prime minister, the minister of justice, the minister of marine, the ex–minister of customs — this government, with positive knowledge, with abundance of proof, that the grossest violations of the customs laws were being perpetrated in this country.

I will not disclose the source of my information and I will say very frankly why. If I were to do so those who are guilty in this matter would be notified within an hour and would be able to take the necessary precautions to cover their tracks. Innocent business men would not dare to walk the streets of Montreal if it were known that they disclosed certain information. Yes, and the ministers know this.

The prime minister was duly informed and aware of these conditions. He knew of them. He was fully advised.

The central, pivotal point, the veritable cesspool of it all is in the great customs district of Montreal. I find running all through this thing like a slimy, evil influence the name of Bisaillon. The worst of crooks, he is the intimate of ministers, the petted favourite of this government. The recipient of a modest salary, he rolls in wealth and opulence, a typical debauched public official. The joke is that this government promoted this man after they had knowledge of his crimes. He had a junior position in the customs service, and he was promoted by the minister of customs — not the present one, but his predecessor — in 1924, to be chief preventive officer of Quebec.

This man has a farm on the boundary, on the Canadian side and on the American side, a rendezvous of noted crooks and smugglers. He is the head, the chief smuggler of the ring, a perjurer and a thief. In the presence of a deputy and another witness, this individual, asking to be appointed to certain positions, offered to superior officers a bribe of

$100 a week. This was reported to the minister of the Crown. Subsequently, the same minister promoted him. Bisaillon offered a bribe for promotion, but "no," this government says, "do not waste your money. We will give you the position without any bribe." They elected this arch smuggler, whose record since 1903 and 1904 is slimy with rottenness and crime, to the most responsible position in the gift of the government in the customs service of this government in the Dominion of Canada as far as an opportunity for corruption, crooked- ness and graft was concerned.

The activities of Bisaillon ran through nearly all the occurrences in connection with the Customs Department in Montreal and district. Let me take, first the barge *Tremblay*. Now this is a typical liquor smuggling case. The barge *Tremblay* was seized at Quebec by the officers of the liquor control board. Bisaillon, the chief Dominion preventive officer, had arranged for the passage of this barge to be smooth and uninterrupted, but the liquor board officers did their duty, for which I give them credit.

Then Bisaillon stepped in with his superior power as chief preven- tive officer, made a seizure over and above the liquor board and took the barge out of their hands. Afterwards, provincial officers arrested Bisaillon and he was put on trial. He was prosecuted. My hon. friend the Solicitor General (Lucien Cannon) was, I think, one of the Crown attorneys in the case.

Bisaillon received moneys from the Crown, some $69,000 discov- ered in some cases. He received tens of thousands of dollars, deposited them to his account, and he never remitted those moneys to the account of the Receiver General. Even in the face of the disclosures in this case, the man was kept on as chief preventive officer. He was not prosecuted nor was any attempt made to recover the moneys which he had stolen and defrauded the government of. He was not released from his office until notice of my resolution on the order paper appeared in the press in November last.

Now, I take another case. The case of two women with two trunks on the Canadian Steamship Company wharf at Montreal. These trunks and these two women came under the suspicion of certain officers and the trunks were finally opened and were found to be filled with narcotic drugs. The Royal Canadian Mounted Police arrested the women and they were convicted. Bisaillon knew these women when he saw them and so did Giroux, another customs officer, a tidewater surveyor, one of the chief officers of customs. Both of them were there and talked with these women. Both of them saw the trunks and knew all about the narcotics. But when the RCMP brought the case up in the courts, both declared under oath that they could not recognize these women. The judge told them that in his opinion they were perjuring themselves.

Now, what happened to these trunks? The trunks were in the custody of the chief constable and were stolen out of his office. Here we get some idea of the character of this man Bisaillon, the chief preventive officer of this government. Here we get some idea of the nature of this ring of criminals operating brazenly and openly, and in the employ of the government. Associated with them are criminals such as Benny Rose, known as Chicago Benny, a typical American gangster. This man was approached by Morel. Morel was one of the five bandits who were hanged last year at Montreal for holding up a bank car. This man was approached by Morel and Farfar, who is doing seven years in the penitentiary, to induce him to steal the trunks, and to undertake to do so on a certain day. But the gang under the control of Bisaillon beat him to it by twenty-four hours and stole the trunks.

But that is not the whole story. One Bud Harris, a coloured man, who was one of the gang implicated in all this rascality, had $3,000 coming to him and they would not pay him. He then intimated that he was going to disclose the smuggling gang and what happened to him? If you will turn back the files of the Montreal papers, you will find where the body of a coloured man was found wired up and weighted with weights in the Back River. That was the body of Bud Harris. With the knowledge of these things, with the knowledge of the character of this man Bisaillon, with the knowledge of these activities of Giroux and others, this government preserved them in their office since last February. And then this government comes to this House and asks for confidence!

I am not taking this government by surprise. I have under my hands a letter showing that this matter was before the Privy Council. For 11 months, it has been a vital question before this government and my charge is that nothing has been done, the matter has been neglected, the criminals protected and the fraud on the exchequer continued with the knowledge of the government. I move, seconded by Mr. Manion:

That because of allegations of grave irregularities in the Department of Customs and Excise, no adjournment should be granted until a special committee of seven members is appointed to investigate thoroughly the administration of the department. ◀

If anything, a parliamentary recess was even more pressing for the Liberals, but Georges-Henri Boivin, the member for Shefford and minister of customs and excise, had little choice. He replied to Stevens as best he could, by chastising the member for waiting until that night to raise the controversy. Unimpressed, Conservative John Stansell (Norfolk-Elgin) attempted what his colleague from Oxford North had failed to achieve, by moving the adjournment of the debate. Incredibly, the motion to adjourn was rejected by a single vote, 119–118. Five Progressive members had voted with the Conservatives, against the counsel of their new leader, Robert Forke.

In the coming days, procedural motions came fast and furious. Throughout, the Liberal minority held. Boivin finally conceded to a special parliamentary committee of inquiry and managed to remove the Customs Scandal from the House order paper — for now. The debate dragged on until, on March 3, the vote on the throne speech was put to the Commons and passed 111–102. The long-awaited adjournment was at hand.

THE KING–BYNG THING
▶▶▶▶▶▶▶▶▶▶▶▶▶

PRINCE ALBERT, Saskatchewan had elected Liberal candidate Charles Macdonald in the 1925 general election, with a majority of 2,663 over the Conservative candidate, a 30-year-old Prince Albert lawyer named John Diefenbaker.

Macdonald's parliamentary career was unique. He offered his seat to King before he had a chance to sit in the House. King promised to reward him with a Senate seat, but it was 1935 before King kept his promise. Ill health prevented Macdonald from being sworn in, and he never attended a single session of the Senate. Macdonald was the only person ever elected to the House of Commons and appointed to the Senate who never sat in either.

Neither Diefenbaker nor any Progressive candidate contested the Prince Albert seat against King in the February 15 by-election. Although an independent candidate dared to share the ballot with the prime minister, King won handily.

On Monday, March 15, 1926, the right honourable member for Prince Albert was escorted down the floor of the House by his ministers Ernest Lapointe and William Motherwell. His entry brought the standings in the House of Commons to 116 Conservatives, 101 Liberals, 25 Progressives and three others.

Soon, the sensational revelations of the House of Commons committee investigating the Department of Customs and Excise was again threatening King's tenuous Liberal minority. The Liberal chair, Paul Mercier, tabled on June 18 a report that left the government unscathed, although it was harsh in its criticism of the former customs minister, Senator Jacques Bureau. Stevens rose on June 22 and admonished the report, offering an amendment that unequivocally censured the government in its handling of corruption in the Customs Department. The opposition's final assault had begun.

At 5:15 a.m., Saturday, June 26, 1926, the prime minister was given a brief reprieve. Liberal and Progressive amendments, sub-amendments and motions to adjourn were fiercely tabled and debated; anything and everything was done to prevent a vote on the motion of censure. Finally, a government motion to adjourn passed with a majority of one. King then realized that his alliance with the Progressive members was no longer reliable. He decided to dissolve Parliament and face the country. This way, he would have the machinery of the federal public service behind him during the election.

No one in Ottawa was aware of what transpired between King and Governor General the Baron Byng except the two men themselves. After two days of confidential negotiations, it became clear that Byng did not want to dissolve Parliament while a motion of censure lay unresolved in the House. The Conservatives, Byng argued with his indignant prime minister, had the most members in the House and Opposition Leader Meighen should at least be given the opportunity to form a government.

On Monday, June 28, King walked into Byng's office and handed the Governor General an order in council requesting an election writ. Byng refused. In shock and anger, the prime minister tendered his resignation, which Byng accepted. King left Byng's office, and the Governor General sent for Arthur Meighen.

Minutes before two o'clock, a messenger found Meighen and delivered the Governor General's summons. Meighen opted to attend the sitting of Parliament and visit Byng later. The curtain had fallen on the King–Byng Thing. But on June 28, 1926, for a few moments of debate in the House of Commons, Canada had no prime minister.

► **RIGHT HON. WILLIAM LYON MACKENZIE KING** (Prince Albert): Mr. Speaker, I have a very important announcement which I wish to make to the House before proceeding any further. The public interest demands a dissolution of this House of Commons. As prime minister, I so advised His Excellency the Governor General shortly before noon today. His Excellency having declined to accept my advice to grant a dissolution, to which I believe under British practice I was entitled, I immediately tendered my resignation which His Excellency has been graciously pleased to accept. In the circumstances, as one of the members of the House of Commons, I would move that the House do now adjourn.

RIGHT HON. ARTHUR MEIGHEN — Leader of the Opposition (Portage la Prairie): Mr. Speaker, if I caught the prime minister's words aright, they were that the House adjourn. That the government has resigned. I wish to add only this: that I am . . .

MR. KING: I might say that this motion is not debatable.

MR. MEIGHEN: I do not propose to debate it, but I presume that the prime minister will agree that I have a right to make a statement. As the House knows, we are close to the end of the session and the question of how the session should be finished is one of great importance to the country. I think there should be a conference between myself and the prime minister.

MR. KING: May I make my position clear? At the present time there is no government. I am not prime minister. I cannot speak as prime minister. I can speak only as one member of this House, and it is as a humble member of this House that I submit that insomuch as His Excellency is without an adviser, I do not think it would be proper for the House to proceed to discuss anything. ◄

"Never before, in the history of this country or of any part of the British Empire," Meighen later recalled, "had a ministry left its country without a government at all."

The House adjourned immediately after King's statement and Meighen had a chance to respond to the Governor General's invitation. Meighen weighed declining the invitation, thus causing another federal election in less than a year. Alternatively, he could not hold the Progressive vote for long, if at all. He would have to name a cabinet, but the new privy councillors would have to resign their seats and seek re-election in a by-election, pursuant to legislation then in existence. It would be a long chess game with Mr. King. One that Meighen would lose.

In the public galleries on that historic June day could be found the observant faces of two young men sitting in on the debate: 29-year-old Mike Pearson and 23-year-old Paul Martin. Thirty years later, the two men would battle for the leadership of King's Liberal party.

ARTHUR MEIGHEN'S GAMBLE
▶▶▶▶▶▶▶▶▶▶▶▶▶▶▶▶▶▶

ALL AFTERNOON and into the evening of Monday, June 28, 1926, the Right Hon. Arthur Meighen wrestled with Governor General Byng's invitation to form a government. He studied political advice from former prime minister Robert Borden and summoned the deputy minister of justice. Finally, he accepted. But as King had certainly calculated, the Independence of Parliament Act would doom any chance Meighen had of preventing, sooner or later, a negative vote in the House. Under the act, any member not a minister of the Crown when elected, and becoming one after, must resign his seat in the Commons and seek re-election. For Meighen, this meant that as soon as he named a cabinet, all appointed ministers would lose their seats until a by-election could be held. Meanwhile, the loss of the seats would seriously hinder the prime minister's ability to prevent a vote of non-confidence in the House. It was clear to Meighen that King was not amenable to any adjournment so as to allow his cabinet members or the new prime minister to be re-elected.

Meighen decided to appoint seven "acting" ministers, who would receive no pay but have full powers and responsibilities over departments. On paper, it was ingenious. Meighen could not be "acting prime minister." He lost his front-row seat in the Commons and from then on could only watch and pass notes down from the members' lobby.

From his new seat on the opposition side of the House, Mackenzie King did not make the new prime minister wait long. On June 30, budgetary motions were tabled and the House went

into committee of the whole. A number of small items were brought forward, and aside from the occasional minor query on points of detail there was no early indication of what was to follow — until $1.66 million was requested for "non permanent active militia."

The government House leader was Sir Henry Drayton, who, according to orders in council that would later be tabled, was "minister without portfolio but responsible for the Department of Finance and Railways." Through the machinations of Meighen, Drayton was sitting in the cabinet seats of the Commons solely on the basis of a Privy Council oath he had taken in 1919, when he had been appointed minister of finance in the Union cabinet of Sir Robert Borden.

▶ **WILLIAM L. MACKENZIE KING** — Leader of the Opposition (Prince Albert): We are now voting large sums of money to different hon. gentlemen opposite who are supposed to be administering departments of the government. I would like to ask my hon. friend who is leading the House whether he has taken any oath of office.

SIR HENRY DRAYTON — Minister without Portfolio (York West): All the formalities prescribed in the office of the Privy Council have been observed. I do not know how many there are.

MR. KING: I want this information before we vote public money. I ask my hon. friend whether he has taken any oath of office this year.

MR. DRAYTON: No.

MR. KING: Will my hon. friend tell me what department he is administering?

MR. DRAYTON: So far as this is concerned, I have taken all the oaths which go with the administration and with the standing one has as a member of the King's Privy Council.

MR. KING: Those of us sitting on this side who composed the former government have taken the oath as privy councillors, but that does not entitle us to administer departments of the government at present. What I am concerned about is the oath taken when one becomes a minister of the Crown.

HUGH GUTHRIE — Minister without Portfolio (Wellington South): That is not the oath we have taken. None of us are ministers of departments, but merely acting ministers.

MR. KING: Perhaps I could shorten the questions by asking my hon. friend whether all of the acting ministers have been appointed acting ministers by order in council.

MR. DRAYTON: The practice has been the same, I think, in every case.

MR. KING: My hon. friend says that these orders in council were passed in council. Who were in council at the time these orders were passed?

MR. DRAYTON: My hon. friend is now asking a question which he himself on previous occasions said could not be answered.

MR. KING: The country is entitled to know by what authority hon. gentlemen opposite are asking this country to vote millions of dollars for them to administer. It happens to be my duty as leader of His Majesty's loyal opposition to ease the country's mind where there is any doubt on that question.

AN HON. MEMBER: You eased the country's mind the other day!

MR. KING: I would like to ask my hon. friend to tell the House how, when the right hon. gentleman assumed the position of prime minister, he complied with the constitutional rule which requires a quorum of four to enable any order in council to be passed to appoint any minister.

MR. DRAYTON: I did not count how many were present but my recollection is that there were six members present.

MR. KING: Privy councillors are not permitted to walk into the council chamber, sit around the table and pass whatever orders they may like, to give each other official positions. If that were the case there is no reason why my erstwhile colleagues and myself should not have walked into the council chamber and assign positions to ourselves that would enable us to control the expenditure of public moneys. The fact that we are members of His Majesty's Privy Council gives us no right whatever to be ministers or acting ministers of the Crown.

We have voted some thousands of dollars already just to see how calmly they would take the process, and how rapidly they are prepared to vote millions of dollars to themselves without having any authority whatever to ask this House for a single dollar!

I submit that what has been disclosed tonight bears out what I said at the time I first decided to advise dissolution. I had in mind a vision of precisely the spectacle we see here tonight. The whole struggle throughout the centuries has been to bring about a system of responsible government whereby every executive act of the Crown should be performed upon the advice of a responsible ministry. Do hon. gentlemen opposite pretend to be such a ministry?

SOME HON. MEMBERS: Sure!

MR. KING: Sure?! It only shows how ignorant hon. gentlemen are of the nature of responsible government. Does my hon. friend who is leading the House think that the people of Canada will be satisfied for one moment with a government constituted as this one is?

MR. DRAYTON: I can only say to my hon. friend that I should like the sensible people of this country to see him at this moment.

ERNEST LAPOINTE (Quebec East): Keep cool, boys. It is only beginning.

MR. KING: If at the instance of one individual, a prime minister can be put into office and with a ministry which is not yet formed be permitted to vote all the supplies necessary to carry on the government of Canada for a year, we have reached a condition in this country which threatens constitutional liberty, freedom and rights in all parts of the world.

LEON LADNER (Vancouver South): Will the right hon. gentleman state frankly and directly to the House who that individual is? Has he the courage?

LUCIEN CANNON (Dorchester): That is Arthur Meighen! Didn't you understand?

MR. KING: I beg my hon. friend's pardon. I ask him, how does the present prime minister come to be in office?

MR. LADNER: By a proper constitutional course. Owing to the lack of confidence of the majority of the members of the House, due to the dereliction of duty of the former government.

MR. KING: My hon. friend is mistaken. The government of which I had the honour to be the head never met with defeat from the day that it came into office to the day that it resigned.

AMBROSE BURY (Edmonton East): Mr. Chairman, the right hon. gentleman said a minute ago that the prime minister at the instance of one individual was allowed to get into power.

AN HON. MEMBER: Listen again! You are dreaming!

MR. KING: If hon. gentlemen opposite will not get so excited.

AN HON. MEMBER: Name the individual!

MR. KING: The individual to whom I refer has, I believe, acted according to his conscience, honestly, sincerely, truly. I have nothing disrespectful to say of him in any particular.

MR. BURY: Mr. Chairman, I rise on a point of order. The right hon. leader of the opposition is referring to the action of His Excellency. I do not think he has any right to discuss it.

MR. KING: My hon. friend was seeking to have me name an individual and I am replying. I ask anyone on the other side of the House to stand up and tell hon. members of one single utterance of mine which was disrespectful to the Governor General!

Now, may I say something which I tried to say two or three times this afternoon when I was interrupted but which I think I am free to say now. I have no objection that the right hon. gentleman who is today prime minister of Canada should ge given his chance, if you wish to call it such, to carry on the business of this country at present. I do say, however, that when he took the responsibility of His Excellency's refusal to grant a dissolution he put himself under the necessity of making very clear to this country that in doing so, he is capable of doing all that it involved, and which was that he would be able to conduct the affairs of this country, in this Parliament, in a manner benefiting the honour and dignity of the venerable institution of Parliament. If he is unable to do that, it is then his duty to return to His Excellency and tell His Excellency that he has not been able to carry out his undertaking.

I say that it is not to the honour of the Crown that he should seek to put into the seats of the ministry a group of gentlemen not one of whom has taken any oath of office, and call that the responsible ministry which is to advise His Excellency the Governor General with respect to all the affairs of this country. I cannot think of any act more irresponsible or unconditional than that.

For one hundred years in Great Britain, there is not a single instance of a prime minister having asked for a dissolution and having been refused it. Since this Dominion was formed, since Confederation in 1867, there is not a single instance where a prime minister has advised a dissolution and has been refused it.

JOHN CLARK (Vancouver-Burrard): We have never had a usurper before.

MR. KING: You have certainly got one now in the seat of the prime minister, and one who is more or less of an expert as a usurper.

I say, Mr. Chairman, that at this time we have at heart the interests not only of Canada, but of South Africa, of Australia, of New Zealand, of Newfoundland, of the Irish Free State, of India, yes, and of the British Isles themselves.

THOMAS CANTLEY (Pictou): The United States, too!

MR. KING: No. Not the United States. That shows again how ignorant my hon. friend is. The United States has an entirely different form of government.

I think the only thing benefiting the dignity and the honour of the House, at the moment, is that the hon. member opposite who is leading the House should not attempt to proceed further. I move that the House adjourn; I would first move that the Chairman do now leave the chair. ◄

King's procedural motion was defeated 101–80, but he had driven wedges of doubt into the new government's legitimacy.

Surprisingly, King had had no idea that the day would turn out as well as it did. He later recalled: "It must have been the spirit of my grandfather working through me which caused me to press on and to continue speaking though with no preparation and finally getting the situation so developed as to have rallied all our forces in Parliament and brought the real issue concretely to the fore in a manner which made impossible Meighen's carrying on; completely exposing the hollow pretence and rottenness of the whole proceeding."

The House staggered on and finally adjourned at 1:10 a.m. Later that day, the Conservatives tried to rally and presented long legal arguments in support of the ministry. But Liberal member James Robb (Chateauguay-Huntington) responded by tabling a formal motion that declared that "the actions in this House of the hon. members who have acted as ministers of the Crown since the 29th of June, 1926, are a violation and an infringement of the privileges of this House for the following reasons: that the hon. gentlemen have no right to sit in this House, and should have vacated their seats if they legally hold office; that if they do not hold such office legally they have no right to control the business of government in this House and to ask for supply for the departments of which they state they are acting ministers."

It was just past midnight when Speaker Rudolphe Lemieux (Gaspé) called in the members for the vote. Thomas Bird, the Progressive member representing the riding of Nelson, was paired with Donald Kennedy, an absent member prepared to support the government on the motion. (Under the unofficial practice of pairing, absent or ill members could contract with a member of the other party, who would then abstain. In exchange, the absent member would agree to abstain at some future date to accommodate the absence of the "pair." This gave members greater flexibility in their attendance without risking the management of the House essential to the government whip, whose job it was to ensure that a majority of members were always available when a vote was called. But it was an honour system and was neither sanctioned nor recognized under the rules of the House.)

According to one historian, Bird was "dozing" when the vote was called and "was roused as the House was being counted." When the clerk counted 96 members in favour of Robb's motion, the government whip knew something was amiss; he had expected only 95 yeas. When the nays were counted, Bird made no effort to withdraw his yea vote. It was only after the vote was counted, after the Speaker had declared the motion carried, that Bird rose. "I wish to explain to the House, and with extreme regret, that I was paired with the hon. member for Peace River and I cast my vote inadvertently."

But the Speaker reminded the House of procedural authorities stating clearly that there was no parliamentary recognition of pairing. "The hon. member having voted," concluded Lemieux, "the vote must stand."

The precedence of a pair misdemeanour quickly paled compared with the other political events the Byng–King Affair was causing. For the first time in Canadian history, a government had been defeated by a vote in the House of Commons. King protested that a Governor General had never before refused a prime minister a dissolution. Referring to Meighen, he also claimed that never had one individual attempted to single-handedly act as cabinet. Meighen countered that it was unheard of for a prime minister to abandon the office of prime minister, effectively leaving the country without government. It was an era of political accusation and parliamentary precedent.

Cornered and defeated in the House, Meighen called on the Governor General, and the Fifteenth Parliament was mercifully dissolved. King's reversal of fortune would soon be complete. Robert Forke resigned as leader of the Progressive party on June 30, unable to command party discipline or solidarity. The Progressive party would never again be a force in Canadian politics.

Armed with this disunity in the second-largest opposition party, King took to the hustings a confident man. Before long, he was using Byng's decision as proof positive of the continued interference of British officials in the internal affairs of Canada. Meighen refused to bring the Governor General's name into the campaign, in spite of desperate pleas from his advisers. "I am not getting down to that level," he replied.

The victory was soon consummated. Arthur Meighen lost his Portage la Prairie seat to a Liberal candidate and would never again sit in the House of Commons. When the final returns were in from the September 14 election, the Progressive party had been reduced to 13 seats. The Liberals had 116 seats and the Tories only 91. Before long, the 52-year-old Meighen resigned as leader of the Conservative party. King would reign as prime minister of Canada for seventeen of the next twenty-two years.

SEND FOR MY HONOURABLE FRIEND
▶▶▶▶▶▶▶▶▶▶▶▶▶▶▶▶▶▶▶▶▶▶▶

THE **DOUKHOBORS** were a religious sect and had emigrated en masse from Russia at the turn of the century. First settling in Saskatchewan, most Doukhobors later moved to southern British Columbia. Of the splinter groups that developed, one was particularly fanatical. The Sons of Freedom, as they called themselves, sometimes protested by holding nude parades. A number of their female members had even stripped at a public election meeting in Trail, British Columbia.

This did not escape the attention of Parliament nor of Conservative member and former publisher of the *Trail News*, William Esling. On June 8, 1928, Esling asked the government to consider the deportation of the "radical fanatics."

▶ **CHARLES DUNNING** — Minister of Railways and Canals (Regina): Having had some association with that small minority of the Doukhobors in my own province, may I say in all fairness to the thousands of good citizens and members of the universal brotherhood known as the Doukhobors, which is a religious body with very high principles, that to label them all with the sins committed by a few people in Saskatchewan some years ago, or in British Columbia today would be distinctly unfair.

RICHARD BENNETT — Leader of the Opposition (Calgary South): Is it correct to say that the so-called fanatics, not using that word offensively at all, do not become naturalized?

MR. DUNNING: I think perhaps my hon. friend may be right. I remember on a previous occasion I had reason to look into the matter of deportation. Immediately the question arose having regard to the changes which have taken place in the country from which they came.

WILLIAM ESLING (Kootenay West): My references were to religious fanatics who today are offending the public by exhibitions of absolute nakedness.

The prime minister laughs?! I ask him a question. What would he do some morning out at Kingsmere if he were to arise, go out and find on his verandah a half a dozen Doukhobor women totally devoid of all clothing? What would he do?

RIGHT HON. WILLIAM L. MACKENZIE KING — Prime Minister (Prince Albert): I would send for my right hon. friend, the leader of the opposition!

MR. BENNETT: As usual, the prime minister exaggerates. Dispensing patronage outside of his own party has never been characteristic of him at any time! ◄

The published version of Hansard records the conversation differently, omitting the references to "Kingsmere" and "women." It also added "and the leader of the Progressive party" to King's response and reworded Bennett's reply to read: "There would be a riot if you overlooked your own supporters."

Both Gratton O'Leary and John Diefenbaker chastised Hansard stenographers for editing the exchange. But in fairness, it was undoubtedly changed at the prime minister's request.

Even the tamer version as it now appears in Hansard remains evidence of the extraordinary and rare exchange between two elderly celibates, neither known for having a sense of humour.

7
At War
▶▶▶▶▶▶▶▶▶

THE "RUTHLESS" COOPERATIVE COMMONWEALTH
▶▶▶▶▶▶▶▶▶▶▶▶▶▶▶▶▶▶▶▶▶▶▶▶▶▶▶▶▶▶▶▶▶▶

THE COOPERATIVE COMMONWEALTH FEDERATION emerged as a viable political organization during the winter of 1931, just as the Great Depression was at its worst. James Shaver Woodsworth, from his caring perch in Ottawa, was a friendly and ready listener to many a poor, unemployed Canadian. So were the Labour and United Farmers of Alberta members of the House. Before long, Woodsworth was chairing meetings of a "cooperative group" of MPs. In January, the UFA called for a conference of cooperating groups.

The conference was held in Calgary in August 1932 and quickly coalesced into a common desire to form a national political party. Woodsworth suggested the name of Canadian Commonwealth Federation, but there were other proposals, such as the Socialist Party of Canada and the United Workers' Commonwealth. In the end, a compromise was worked out: the Cooperative Commonwealth Federation. Before adjourning, the conference scheduled the first CCF convention in Regina in 1933, and Woodsworth was elected national president. From that point on, the popularity of the CCF would flourish.

Prime Minister Richard Bennett came out swinging. In a speech he gave in Toronto in November 1932, he charged, "This propaganda is being put forward by organizations from foreign lands that seek to destroy our institutions. We ask every man and woman to put the iron heel of ruthlessness against a thing of that kind."

Unimpressed, Woodsworth rose in the House of Commons on February 1, 1933.

▶ **JAMES WOODSWORTH** (Winnipeg North Centre): Mr. Speaker, I move:

> *Whereas the prevalence of the present depression throughout the world indicates fundamental defects in the existing economic system, be it resolved that the government should immediately take measures to the setting up of a cooperative commonwealth in which all natural resources and the socially necessary machinery of production will be used in the interests of the people and not for the benefit of the few.*

Mr. Speaker, we must distinguish between the CCF and communism. It is true that both believe in a changed social order, in a new economic system. The Communists are convinced that this can be brought about only by violence. We believe that it may come in Canada by peaceful methods and in an orderly fashion.

RAYMOND MORAND (Essex East): The end being the same.

MR. WOODSWORTH: It may very well be that force may prove inevitable, yes, if the attitude of certain gentlemen is persisted in and the people of this country are denied the right they have in self-expression and to the enjoyment of a decent livelihood!

We believe that the first step to be taken in bettering the present conditions is to adopt a planned economy. I do not think we could proceed very far without increasing the public control of industry. Industry is in a bad way. I do not believe that the industrialist can pay his dividends today and at the same time pay decent wages. But when that alternative must be decided, I say unhesitatingly that the employees ought to be secured a decent living and their claims should have priority over dividends. If industry as constituted under present conditions cannot grant a decent living to its employees, so much the worse for industry, and in such cases, it should be taken over.

The prime minister in his Toronto speech said: "Are you prepared to give up those things which have been earned by honest toil?" Has the prime minister's own fortune been gained by honest toil?

SOME HON. MEMBERS: Shame! Withdraw!

MR. SPEAKER — George Black (Yukon): The hon. member has made the imputation that the prime minister has been guilty of dishonesty. I would regret to have to name the hon. member, but I propose to do so unless he conforms to the rules of the House. I ask the hon. member to withdraw his objectionable words.

MR. WOODSWORTH: I withdraw any imputation that the prime minister has made his money dishonestly.

Large fortunes have been made in this country by other means than that of the old-fashioned toil. There is no reason why the right to the possession of such fortunes may not be challenged and why, when there are thousands of people on the verge of starvation, there may not be levied on those who presently own them, the large amounts that are necessary to put into effect certain kinds of public works or to make other provision that will adequately meet the needs of the people in this crisis. It is quite constitutional to do that in the case of international war; it is equally constitutional to do it in the case of a war on poverty. We have not paid sufficient attention to the welfare of our fellow citizens. May I be permitted to quote those old lines of Goldsmith, which I think ought to be inscribed in every legislative chamber in Canada:

> *Ill fares the land, to hastening ill a prey*
> *Where wealth accumulates, and men decay.* ◄

Woodsworth's motion was discussed at five sittings of the House. Twenty-seven members voiced their views on the resolution. Among the most fervent foes of the CCF was the Conservative member for West York, J. Earl Lawson. Arguing that the CCF proposal would lead to complete state control, he concluded that "co-operative commonwealth is communism. Communism without bloody revolution, if you will, but, nevertheless, communism."

On February 27, the leader of the opposition, William King, provided a lengthy critique, one that focused on the many practical difficulties with the proposed cooperative federation. "If property is simply to be expropriated, then we should be told about it," he told the House. "On the other hand, if it is not going to be expropriation by force and violence, then it must be assumed that those who are possessed of private property will be remunerated. Where is the money going to come from?"

As soon as King resumed his seat, Dr. Ira Cotnam, the Conservative member for North Renfrew, moved the adjournment of the debate. The motion carried 84–52 and the cooperative commonwealth resolution did not resurface on the order paper.

The debate in the Commons proved to be a moral victory for the fledging CCF. Opposition criticism had taken the form of serious consideration of their party's resolutions, rather than anti-Communist rhetoric. The Cooperative Commonwealth Federation was off and running.

AT WAR, AGAIN
►►►►►►►►►►

THE HORRORS OF the First World War were still fresh in the memories of most Canadians when Parliament was suddenly summoned on September 3, 1939, convening four days later in special session. By the time members from the western and Maritime provinces arrived in Ottawa, German forces had occupied Poland for seven days.

British Prime Minister Neville Chamberlain had warned German leader Adolf Hitler that any incursion into Poland would mean war with England. War with England, in 1939, meant war with Canada. On August 25, as Hitler played his game of military provocation along the Polish border, Prime Minister Mackenzie King sent him and Mussolini telegrams urging them to seek peaceful resolutions to any international problem. "Force is not a substitute for reason," King wrote. But his plea, along with those of many other world leaders, was in vain.

The House met on September 8, 1939, with the sole purpose of declaring war on Germany. On the next day, after the formalities of the opening of a session had been tended to, Dr. Robert Manion, the Conservative leader of the opposition, and Mackenzie King began the record in earnest condemnation of Germany and in favour of an immediate declaration of hostilities between Canada and that country. They hoped that the House would show unanimous consent. It would not.

►**RIGHT HON. WILLIAM L. MACKENZIE KING** — Prime Minister (Prince Albert): I noticed in the press last evening that one of the German papers had quoted Hitler as saying that if England wished to fight, she must remember that if she entered this fight, the prize of victory would be the British Empire. Well, that includes Canada. As my hon. friend has said, there is no portion of the globe which any nation would be likely to covet more than this Dominion of Canada. There is no other portion of the earth's surface that contains such wealth as lies buried here. Nowhere are there such stretches of territory capable of feeding for generations to come — not hundreds of thousands but millions of people. No, Mr. Speaker, the ambition of this dictator is not Poland.

If this conqueror by his methods of force, violence and terror and other ruthless iniquities is able to crush the peoples of Europe, what is going to become of the doctrine of isolation of this North American continent? If Britain goes down, if France goes down, the whole business of isolation will prove to have been a mere myth. There will in time be no freedom on this continent; there will in time be no liberty. Life will not be worth living. It is for all of us on this continent to do our part to save its privileged position by helping others. ◄

The dramatic debate on Canada's entry into the Second World War was most difficult on James Woodsworth. The veteran 65-year-old CCF member was a declared pacifist and could not bring himself to support war under any circumstances.

Unknown but to those closest to him, Woodsworth had suffered a severe stroke only a few days before his speech on

September 8, 1939. Only with the assistance of speaking notes discreetly handed to him by fellow CCFer Tommy Douglas was Woodsworth able to speak in the House. "When he rose to speak, he could hardly see," Douglas later recalled in his biography, *The Road to Jerusalem*. "Mrs. Woodsworth had made a few notes at his dictation — a cue word here and there — and put them on cards in thick crayon letters at least an inch high. I slipped into the seat beside him and handed the cards up to him one by one."

It was a sad, mournful speech by a man who would stand alone on that historic day in the Commons, isolated in conviction from each and every one of his CCF colleagues, including Douglas.

► **JAMES WOODSWORTH** (Winnipeg North Centre): Mr. Speaker, it is only a few months since we erected in Ottawa a memorial to the poor fellows who fell in the last war. It is hardly finished before we are into the next war. After the last war many of us dreamed a great dream of an ordered world, a world to be founded on justice. But unfortunately the covenant of the League of Nations was tied up with the Versailles treaty, which I regard as an absolutely iniquitous treaty. Under that treaty we tried to crush Germany. We imposed indemnities which have been acknowledged by all to be impossible. We took certain portions of territory. Even French black troops were put into the Rhineland — an indignity much resented at the time by the Germans. We took away colonies, sank ships, and all the rest of it. To no small extent it was this kind of treatment which created Hitler. I am not seeking to vindicate the things that Hitler has done — not at all. He may be a very devil incarnate. But you cannot indict a great nation and a great people such as the German people. The fact is we got rid of the kaiser only to create conditions favourable to the development of a Hitler. Canada had her responsibility.

I would ask, did the last war settle anything? It settled nothing and the next war into which we are asked to enter, however big and bloody it may be, is not going to settle anything either. That is not the way in which settlements are brought about. While we are urged to fight for freedom and democracy, it should be remembered that war is the very negation of both. The victor may win. But if he does, it is by adopting the self-same tactics which he condemns in his enemy. Canada must accept her share of responsibility for the existing state of affairs. Canada has shipped enormous quantities of nickel and scrap-iron, copper and chromium to both Japan and Germany. If any shooting is to be done the first people who should face the firing squad are those who have made money out of a potential enemy.

The common people of the country gain nothing by slaughtering the common people of any other country. I cannot give my consent to anything that will drag us into another war. I have every respect for the man who, with a sincere conviction, goes out to give his life if necessary in a cause which he believes is right. But I have just as much respect for the man who refuses to enlist to kill his fellow men and, as under modern conditions, to kill women and children as well, as must be done on every front. These facts ought to be faced.

I envy the courage possessed by the men who go to the front. I envy the Department of War the huge sums that are available when war is on. Why are not these sums available in peace time? Why cannot we have the same kind of venturesome spirit during peace time?

When the call came for us to come to Ottawa, I was staying at a little summer resort near the international boundary south of Vancouver. Near Blaine there is a peace arch between the two countries. The children gathered their pennies and planted a rose garden and they held a fine ceremony in which they interchanged national flags and sang songs and that kind of thing; a beautiful incident.

I take my place with the children. I know it seems very foolish. I do not care whether you think me an impossible idealist or a dangerous crank. I am going to take my place beside the children and those young people, because it is only as we adopt new policies that this world will be at all a liveable place for our children who follow us.

We laud the courage of those who go to the front. Yes, I have boys of my own and I hope they are not cowards. But if any of those boys, not from cowardice but really through belief, is willing to take his stand on this matter and, if necessary, to face a concentration camp or a firing squad, I shall be more proud of that boy than if he enlisted for the war!

GEORGE TUSTIN (Prince Edward-Lennox): Shame!

MR. WOODSWORTH: The hon. member can say "shame" but that is my belief.

Now you can hammer me as much you like. I must thank the House for the great courtesy shown me. I rejoice that it is possible to say these things in a Canadian Parliament under British institutions. It would not be possible in Germany, I recognize that. But it is possible here, and I want to maintain the very essence of our British institutions of real liberty. I believe that the only way to do it is by an appeal to the moral forces which are still resident among our people, and not to resort to brute force. ◄

Three Quebec members joined Woodsworth in his dissent, but their four voices stood alone and lonely in a House that roared for war against Hitler.

On Sunday, September 10, 1939, a proclamation signed by Governor General Tweedsmuir, King and Attorney General Ernest Lapointe was published in a special edition of the *Canada Gazette*. "We do hereby declare and proclaim," the *Gazette* read, "that a state of war with the German Reich exists and has existed in our Dominion of Canada as and from the tenth day of September, 1939."

SURPRISE DISSOLUTION
►►►►►►►►►►►►►►

ON MANY OF THE MOST critical matters of state, a prime minister must decide alone, sometimes against the advice of his most trusted advisers. By 1940, Mackenzie King had mastered the art of prime ministership. If ever there was an example of his political leadership, the sudden dissolution of 1940 was it.

Of the many traditions of Parliament, providing the leader of the opposition with an advance copy of the speech from the throne is considered sacrosanct. Dr. Robert Manion should have guessed that something was amiss when, even as he stood in the Senate chamber listening to the Governor General, he had yet to receive a copy.

King had promised the new Conservative leader that there would be a full session of Parliament in 1940 before any general election was called. Under conditions of world war, the expectations were that King would table a motion to extend the life of the Eighteenth Parliament, as had been done by Borden and Laurier in 1916. For what other reason would he suddenly convene from across the country 245 members of the House of Commons and 96 senators?

King's machinations were a result of several factors quite out of his control. The first occurred in the fall of 1939. Quebec premier Maurice Duplessis had called a provincial election, clamouring that federal war measures intruded upon provincial jurisdictions. In Ottawa, King's Quebec cabinet colleagues told Quebec voters that they would resign if Duplessis won. Duplessis was soundly trounced.

Then, the Liberal premier of Ontario, Mitchell Hepburn, declared that the federal government was not contributing enough towards the war effort. King and Hepburn knew each other. As a rookie Liberal member of the House in 1926, Hepburn had been given the most remote seat in the House of Commons. "If his assigned desk were any further removed from the government's front bench," explains Neil McKenty in a biography of Hepburn, "he would have been out in the lobby. Hepburn was outraged." Hepburn even threatened to sit on the opposition side but his complaints fell on deaf ears. For eight years, King ignored the ambitious young member and never offered him a cabinet post.

The result of the Quebec election, the opportunity of playing Hepburn against the war effort and the possibility of holding the election before war casualties began in earnest convinced King that the time was ripe to call an election.

The only individuals who knew what the Governor General was about to announce in the speech from the throne were King's Quebec political colleague and Justice Minister Ernest Lapointe, Speaker Pierre Casgrain and of course King. On January 25, 1940, the jaws of Liberal cabinet and caucus members dropped in unison with those of opposition party members as Lord Tweedsmuir (John Buchan), the Governor General, announced "an immediate appeal to the country." King then rose.

► **RIGHT HON. WILLIAM L. MACKENZIE KING** — Prime Minister (Prince Albert): Mr. Speaker, I rise to move the House do now adjourn, but if the House will permit me so I should like to make a statement to hon. members. The House will recall that at the special session my hon. friend the leader of the opposition asked me if I was prepared to give an undertaking that an election would not be called by the present government before Parliament had again been summoned. I should like to read to the House the words used, found at page 157 of Hansard:

> *As to the question of a general election before another session, my hon. friend has been kind enough to say that I told him some time ago that I would not think of anything of the kind or countenance it.*

But as hon. members know, just a week ago yesterday, the premier of the largest province in this country . . .

AGNES MACPHAIL (Grey Bruce): A Liberal!

MR. KING: . . . introduced in the Ontario legislature a resolution which was directed in no uncertain terms at the government of Canada now administering its affairs. That resolution was seconded by the leader of the Conservative opposition in the Ontario legislature. When the legislature adopted the resolution and it was given a permanent place on the records of the legislature, quite a different situation presented itself to this government. May I read the resolution?

> . . . *that the federal government at Ottawa has made so little effort to prosecute Canada's duty in the war in the vigorous manner the people of Canada desire to see.*

It is a charge against the federal government. Since war was declared, and this Parliament decided that Canada would participate in the war — decided in the unanimous manner in which it did — my colleagues and myself have given every ounce of our strength and every hour of our time in the most devoted manner possible endeavouring to further Canada's war effort. We have not tried to do so in a dramatic or spectacular way.

Already, after this resolution is passed, the leader of the Conservative party in Ontario, at a political meeting, tells the meeting that the election must start at once. He gives them the slogan "King must go." I am quite willing to accept that slogan if he will add the words "to the country."

It is now evident that a political campaign has begun. I ask members whether it is wise to try to carry on a political campaign in the country and a political campaign in this Parliament — two campaigns at one and the same time — while war is going on at the front.

This Parliament was returned in 1935 and this is 1940. That in itself, in my opinion, is the strongest reason why there should be an election at this time. If an election is to take place, is it not wise to have it just as soon as we possibly can?

MISS MACPHAIL: In the winter?

MR. KING: What about the men who are fighting overseas? They have to face the winter!

MISS MACPHAIL: I should like to see them drive over the roads!

MR. KING: An election will take nearly eight weeks. Provided we have a dissolution in the very near future, we might have the election over before the end of March. The roads will not have broken up.

MISS MACPHAIL: They will be piled up, fence-high!

MR. KING: I do not care what time of the year an election is held! There will always be some objections to consider. April will not be a month for an election. Nor will May.

I have had to face, and my colleagues have had to face, the probability of a great offensive on the Western Front taking place in the spring. What I am proposing at the moment is not to extend my time of office, or that of my colleagues, but solely to allow the people of this country to say, as they are entitled to say, whom they wish to carry on their government during this very critical time.

The government intends to make provision for the military vote being taken overseas, and will do that under the War Measures Act.

ROBERT MANION — Leader of the Opposition (London): That is the way Hitler would do it!

ERNEST LAPOINTE — Minister of Justice (Quebec East): Hitler does not take votes.

MR. KING: I should like to read what President Lincoln had to say with respect to the election which took place under his administration during the period of the civil war. The volume I have in my hand is one which was given to me by Lady Laurier. It was taken from Sir Wilfrid Laurier's library after Sir Wilfrid's death.

. . . The election along with its incidental and undesirable strife, has done good too. It had demonstrated that a people's government can sustain

*a national election in the midst of a great civil war. It shows, also, how
sound and strong we still are.*

Mr. Speaker, our strength is being impaired by those who seek to create
in the public mind distrust concerning both our ability and our
patriotic efforts. There is only one national authority higher than
Parliament. That is the people themselves whose servants as members
of Parliament we all are.

We are in the midst of the worst situation this world has ever
known and I am afraid the situation is going to get worse and worse.
No one can say how long this war will last. It may be three years; it
may be longer. There appears to be a danger of war spreading over
vaster areas than were ever thought of before it began. So may I say
that if we have to carry the grave responsibility of office in war and at
a time of war such as at the present, then we must be fortified by the
voice of this country, expressed in no uncertain terms. Leave it to the
people of Canada to say whom they wish to carry on the government
of Canada in this period of world war. I move, Mr. Speaker, that the
House do now adjourn.

MR. MANION: Mr. Speaker . . .

MR. KING: The motion is not before the House.

MR. MANION: No one is to be allowed to say anything in reply to
the prime minister's prepared speech? Is it the intention to gag this
House? Is the prime minister to come before this House and make a
prepared speech, of which no hint was given to anyone, and then
attempt to close the mouths of the rest of us? I ask him if he dares that.

MR. KING: If my hon. friend wished to speak, I should be quite
pleased to have him do so.

MR. MANION: In the first place, Mr. Speaker, I should like it
distinctly pointed out that there is no particular courtesy in permitting
me to speak, any more than permitting the prime minister to speak
on a motion which is not debatable. I should like to point out also that
the custom in the Parliament of Canada has always been for the
government to give a copy of the speech from the throne to the leader
of the opposition an hour or so in advance. No such courtesy was
extended today, not even up to the time when you, Mr. Speaker, had
the copy of the speech in your hands. Until I went into the Senate
chamber I had absolutely no hint that there was any thought of

anything like this. The prime minister brought members here from the four corners of Canada apparently to dissolve the House tonight. It is so unprecedented to treat an opposition in this manner. He prepares a political speech to be delivered here this afternoon and gives no one else an opportunity of preparing any remarks in advance.

MR. KING: Will my hon. friend allow me to say one word? He will realize that a speech from the throne containing a declaration of an immediate appeal to the country was a document that had to be kept very secret. Otherwise, as my hon. friend knows, that information would have been on the streets of this country before it was announced in Parliament.

MR. MANION: The right hon. gentleman merely adds insult to injury. He suggests that if he had given me a copy of the speech I would have blathered it all over the streets. As a matter of a fact, I have no doubt that the press had copies of the speech before it was read in the Senate.

To put over a political trick of this kind is disgraceful and is sneering at the political traditions of Canada and the British Empire. Why did he not discuss the matters in confidence with me and with the leaders of the other parties in this House?

You cannot turn on a radio without hearing the words of some minister of the government who is putting out what is supposedly a description of Canada's war effort, but about two-thirds of those speeches are political propaganda. We showed a desire to play ball, but the present procedure on the part of the prime minister shows an inexcusable desire to play politics instead. In other words, instead of preparing for the war, they were preparing for an election.

I say that it is the duty of the prime minister and his government to come before Parliament and give an account of their stewardship. So far as I am concerned, I think Mr. Hepburn is right. I think he has been right all along. And never was I so sure that he is right as I am now made sure by this piece of political trickery of the prime minister today.

MR. KING: Never was there a more responsible act!

MR. MANION: If it is the decision of the prime minister to dissolve the House tonight, we shall leave it in the mouths of the people to say which party they want to govern them and to carry on Canada's war effort. I am convinced that not only the prime minister but his government will be swept out of power.

JAMES WOODSWORTH (Winnipeg North Centre): Mr. Speaker. I rise to a point of order.

MR. SPEAKER: The motion before the House is not debatable. The hon. member can proceed only with the unanimous consent of the House. Has the hon. member the unanimous consent of the House?

SOME HON. MEMBERS: Yes.

MR. WOODSWORTH: Mr. Speaker, almost for the first time in my political life, I find myself very nearly in complete agreement with the leader of the opposition.

The prime minister talks about free speech. One of my own sons came back the other day from Scotland. He said to me: "You know, it is astonishing. As soon as I landed on the shores of Canada, I felt that in some way the people of Canada had been frightened, were afraid to speak out what they thought." There is literature published in Great Britain and coming to this country that is banned in this Dominion. It is a ridiculous situation. Are we to become so subservient that we have a virtual dictatorship set up in this country?

As I look across at the prime minister, he does not look like a dictator . . .

MISS MACPHAIL: But he acts like one.

MR. WOODSWORTH: . . . he does not speak like one, but he is acting like a dictator today. ◄

After Woodsworth's remarks, the House took recess. Later that night, a proclamation signed by Lord Tweedsmuir was communicated to all members. The Eighteenth Parliament was dissolved.

The election campaign was a disaster for Robert Manion. On January 26, the Conservative caucus shed their Conservative name and decided to campaign as a "National Government." Instantly, the Quebec vote was lost as the French-Canadians recalled the difficult memories of Borden's Union Government — a government that had enforced conscription.

Two months later, Canadians returned the Liberals to power with what was at the time the largest majority in Canadian history, electing Liberals in 178 of Canada's 245 constituencies. Manion suffered defeat in his own riding. So did King's other heckler on that January day in the Commons, CCF candidate Agnes MacPhail.

The prime minister's manoeuvres were just in time. Less than a month after the election, Germany invaded Norway and turned its guns on Belgium and France. The war in Europe had begun in earnest.

SOME CHICKEN! SOME NECK!
▶▶▶▶▶▶▶▶▶▶▶▶▶▶▶▶▶▶▶

THE ATTENDANCE of the prime minister of England in the chamber of the House of Commons of Canada drew most members from planned New Year's celebrations in their distant ridings. One could not help but suspect that the presence of Sir Winston Churchill in the House may well have been a promotional prelude to conscription.

On a cold Ottawa afternoon, December 30, 1941, an undeniable sense of history permeated the corridors of Canada's Parliament. For Allied war strategists, Churchill foremost, victory was now only a matter of careful planning. But expectations could not be raised too much for fear of a reduction in the war effort. On the other hand, there was no harm in arousing Canadians to the military tasks at hand, particularly on the afternoon of New Year's Eve, only three weeks after the Japanese raid on Pearl Harbor.

▶ **RIGHT HON. WINSTON CHURCHILL** — Prime Minister of Great Britain: Mr. Speaker, in a few months, when the invasion season returns, the Canadian army may be engaged in one of the most frightful battles the world has ever seen. Upon the other hand, their presence may help to deter the enemy from attempting to fight such a battle on British soil. Although, Sir, the long routine of training and preparation is undoubtedly trying to men who left prosperous farms and businesses or other responsible civil work, inspired by an eager and ardent desire to fight the enemy, although this is trying to high-mettled temperaments, the value of the service rendered is unquestionable, and the peculiar kind of self-sacrifice involved, will, I am sure, be cheerfully or at least patiently endured.

Sir, we did not make this war. We did not seek it. We did all we could to avoid it. We did too much to avoid it. We went so far in trying to avoid it as to be almost destroyed by it when it broke upon us. But that dangerous corner has been turned, and with every month and every year that passes we shall confront the evil-doers with weapons as plentiful, as sharp and as destructive as those with which they have sought to establish their hateful domination. The people of the British Empire may love peace. They do not seek the lands or wealth of any country. But they are a tough and hardy lot. We have not journeyed all this way across the centuries, across the oceans, across the mountains, across the prairies, because we are made of sugar candy.

We shall never descend to the German and Japanese level. But if anybody likes to play rough we can play rough too. Hitler and his Nazi gang have sown the wind. Let them reap the whirlwind. Neither the length of the struggle nor any form of severity which it may assume shall make us weary or shall make us quit. We have been concerting the united pacts of more than thirty states and nations to fight on in unity together and in fidelity one to another, without any thought except total and final extirpation of the Hitler tyranny, the Japanese frenzy and the Mussolini flop. These gangs of bandits have sought to darken the light of the world, have sought to stand between the common people of all lands and their march forward into their inheritance. They shall themselves be cast into the pit of death and shame.

We cannot for a moment, Sir, afford to relax. On the contrary, we must drive ourselves forward with unrelenting zeal. In this strange, terrible world war there is a place for everyone, man and woman, old and young, hale and halt. Service in a thousand forms is open. There is no room for the dilettante, for the weakling, for the shirker or the sluggard. The mine, the factory, the dockyard, the salt sea waves, the fields to till, the home, the hospital, the chair of the scientist, the pulpit of the preacher — from the highest to the humblest, the tasks are all of equal honour. The enemies ranged against us, coalesced and combined against us, have asked for total war. Let us make sure they get it.

Let us then look back. Sir, we plunged into this war all unprepared because we had pledged our word to stand by the side of Poland, which Hitler had feniously invaded and had soon struck down. Suddenly the explosion of pent-up German strength burst upon Norway, Denmark, Holland and Belgium. All these absolutely blameless neutrals, to most of whom Germany up to the last moment was giving every kind of guarantee and assurance, were overrun and trampled down. The hideous massacre of Rotterdam, where thirty thousand people perished, showed the fierce barbarism in which the German air force revels when, as in Warsaw and later Belgrade, it was able to bomb practically undefended cities.

On top of all this came the French catastrophe and the French nation was dashed into utter and, as it has proved so far, irretrievable confusion. Their generals misled them. When I warned them that Britain would fight on alone, whatever they did, their generals told their prime minister and his divided cabinet, "In three weeks England will have her neck wrung like a chicken."

Some chicken! Some neck!

We have suffered together and we shall conquer together.

Now, Sir, strong forces are at hand. The tide has turned against the hun. Very soon we shall be superior in every form of equipment to those who have taken us at the disadvantage of being but half armed. The Russian armies under their warrior leader Joseph Stalin are waging furious war with increasing success along a thousand-mile front of their invaded country.

But, greatest of all, the mighty republic of the United States has entered the conflict and entered it in a manner which shows that for her there can be no withdrawal except by death or victory.

Everywhere in occupied France, the decent portion of that great people, the French nation, are raising their hands again. Hope is revived in the hearts of a warlike though disarmed race, cradle of revolutionary liberties and scourge of conquerors. Everywhere breaks the dawn and the light spreads, reddish but bright. Here in Canada, where the French language is cherished and spoken, we stand ready and armed to help and welcome this national resurrection.

Let us then, Sir, address ourselves to our task, not in any way underrating its tremendous difficulties and perils, but in good heart and sober confidence, resolved that, whatever the cost, whatever the suffering, we shall stand by one another, true and faithful comrades, and do our duty, God helping us, to the end. ◄

Upon the British prime minister's final words, the House broke into "God Save the Queen" and gave Churchill a resounding three cheers. Churchill's speech was broadcast around the world. His "Some chicken! Some neck!" became yet another of his masterful battle cries shared amongst Allied soldiers.

8

Tempest in the House
▶▶▶▶▶▶▶▶▶▶▶▶▶▶▶▶▶▶▶▶▶▶▶▶▶▶▶▶▶▶▶▶

A STRANGER IN THE HOUSE
▶▶▶▶▶▶▶▶▶▶▶▶▶▶▶▶▶

THE MINISTER OF NATIONAL defence, James Layton Ralston, landed at Ottawa's Rockcliffe airport on October 18, 1944, from an overseas tour of Canadian troops in Europe. Ralston was one of King's star cabinet ministers. Decorated in World War I, Colonel Ralston had served in the Nova Scotia legislature from 1911 to 1920 and had been King's minister of national defence from 1926 to 1930.

As early as June 10, 1942, Prime Minister King had committed his government to "not necessarily conscription but conscription if necessary." Ralston had already stated in the House of Commons that he would "be the judge, so long as he was the minister of national defence, of when, if ever, conscription was required." In October of 1944, the time had come.

On the nineteenth, he attended King's nine-member war cabinet and tabled a report from the chief of staff of the Canadian military headquarters in London. In contrast with earlier reports, this one concluded that additional military personnel were immediately required from Canada. Reinforcements were lacking at fronts in Italy and northwestern Europe. It took the cabinet by complete surprise and suddenly raised the spectre of conscription for overseas service.

Through the National Resources Mobilization Act, 60,000 trained men were employed in Canada in a home defence role.

They had been conscripted but few had come forward to volunteer for overseas service. They were branded "Zombies." Ralston recommended that 16,000 NRMA men be immediately sent overseas. King suggested that perhaps the military requirements could be met through public appeals to the NRMA pool, through voluntary enlistment. Others around the cabinet table suggested breaking up existing units or reducing the Canadian commitment. For two weeks, the battle raged at the cabinet table.

In his book *The Incredible Canadian*, Bruce Hutchison reveals that the turning point came on October 31, when King received a secret memorandum from the minister of veterans affairs, Ian Mackenzie (Vancouver Centre). As a solution to the impasse, Mackenzie urged King to dismiss Ralston and call upon Gen. Andrew McNaughton. McNaughton, adored by the military, was the only person who had a chance at convincing the Zombies to enlist for overseas service.

But for an entirely different reason, the idea struck King as nothing short of politically ingenious. It was well known in Ottawa that some Conservatives were courting McNaughton as a successor to the ineffective new Tory leader, John Bracken.

When Robert Manion lost the 1940 election, his resignation had brought calls for Arthur Meighen to resume the leadership of the Conservative party. Meighen, now 67 and a senator since 1932, accepted but promptly lost his bid to gain re-election to the House. Bracken then replaced Meighen as party leader at a national convention held in Winnipeg in December 1942 and changed the party name to Progressive Conservative to attract what remained of the Progressive party membership and to appeal to the postwar reform spirit of the Canadian electorate. But by October 1944, he had yet to assert himself on any national issue or to enter Parliament. The leadership of the Tories in the Commons was left to Richard Hanson (York-Sunbury) and then, in 1943, to Gordon Graydon (Peel).

King summoned the general to his Laurier Street home and a marriage of convenience was struck. "I do not know what General McNaughton's politics are," King confessed to the House four weeks later.

Before cabinet the next day, King mentioned a letter of resignation that Ralston had signed in 1942. The offer had then been declined by the prime minister and was long forgotten by Ralston. But now he placed the letter on the table. He then mentioned the name of McNaughton as an individual capable of securing the requisite number of NRMA men to volunteer for overseas duty. Ralston simply rose, shook the hands of his colleagues and left the cabinet room never to return. Never before had a Canadian minister been dismissed while cabinet was in session.

The next day, General McNaughton was sworn in as minister of national defence, although he held no seat in Parliament. During the three weeks he had to find willing Zombies, McNaughton failed miserably. General George Pearkes, the commander of a division of NRMA men, convened a rare military press conference on November 20 and set his frustrated officers loose with the press. The message was clear: the Zombies were not signing up. With overseas conscription emerging as the only alternative, King offered to resign, but the cabinet insisted that he stay on. Then, to make matters worse (again, according to Hutchison), McNaughton telephoned King on the morning of November 22 and conveyed the incredible news that the commanders of the army would resign unless conscription was forthcoming.

When the House of Commons reconvened on November 22, 1944, King tabled correspondence between him and Ralston since the cabinet meeting. Then the House leader of the opposition, Gordon Graydon, took the floor. He tried to table a motion calling for the overseas conscription of the entire NRMA force. Speaker James Glen (Marquette) ruled his motion out of order. The stage was set for another historic cabinet meeting.

With conscription now unavoidable, King informed his colleagues that McNaughton had failed and that there appeared to be no alternative but to follow Ralston's original suggestion. Those gathered around the war cabinet table knew that Parliament might well vote against the government if they did not bring forth conscription. King's Quebec lieutenant and minister of justice, Louis St. Laurent, nodded his support of the proposal, and slowly a consensus emerged. It was only when the meeting ended that Charles "Chubby" Power, the minister of national defence for air, informed his colleagues that he, too, was resigning. A battered but almost unanimous cabinet adjourned late in the evening.

Parliament was informed of the decision the next day and King had McNaughton appear on the floor of the House to answer questions. It was baptism by fire.

▶ **RIGHT HON. WILLIAM L. MACKENZIE KING** — Prime Minister (Prince Albert): I desire to read to the House an order in council approved by the Governor General today:

> *Whereas it has now become necessary in order to meet requirements for the reinforcement of the Canadian forces fighting in Europe and in the Mediterranean, to extend the locality of service of personnel called out for service under the National Resources Mobilization Act, 1940;*
>
> *The minister of national defence is hereby authorized and directed to dispatch to the United Kingdom, or the European or Mediterranean operational theatres such personnel and in such numbers as may be approved by the governor in council (the number hereby approved being 16,000) who are serving by reason of their having been called out for service pursuant to the NRMA.*

I ask the permission of the House to table a copy of this order which has been approved today.

RICHARD HANSON (York-Sunbury): Surrender!

MR. SPEAKER — James Glen (Marquette): Order! I ask the Clerk to inform the minister of national defence that he may attend the meeting of the House.

ANDREW MCNAUGHTON — Minister of National Defence: Mr. Speaker, the reason for my being here today is to report to the House of Commons the facts concerning reinforcements for the Canadian Army overseas. I have to be very careful indeed that no word of mine will carry new information of value to the enemy.

We now, both in Italy and in northwest Europe, are up against fortified zones of great depths and strength with every obstacle and device to hamper our advance which the German mind has been able to conceive: heavy concrete emplacements for machine and anti-tank guns, bomb-proof shelters, elaborate roads and railways for rapid transfer of reserves, deeply buried cables, huge dumps of food and ammunition and spares and replacements for guns and tanks and other gear. In siege warfare there is little opportunity for manoeuvre. When we attack we must use vast quantities of shells to crush out of existence wide sections of the enemy's defence and to paralyse his garrisons and so free the way for the advance of infantry closely supported by the fire of mobile guns. The supply of shells is a vital necessity. In siege warfare you have to pay for victory either in shells or the lives of men.

JAMES RALSTON (Prince): You spoke about 5,000 needed to be in the United Kingdom in December. You propose to send 16,000 more. Is that right?

MR. MCNAUGHTON: Yes.

MR. RALSTON: But I ask you whether the 16,000 would see you through until May?

MR. MCNAUGHTON: I can give no undertaking that it will.

HOWARD GREEN (Vancouver South): NRMA men will not be sent overseas if you can possibly avoid it?

MR. MCNAUGHTON: I have no intention of using compulsion except to meet a deficiency and having regard to the purpose we have of maintaining the strength of our armies overseas.

MR. HANSON: Answer the question!

MR. GREEN: Under your policy, men in the home defence army whom you admit have full combat training will not be put into action,

but young lads who have had only five or six weeks of training will be put into action.

HUMPHREY MITCHELL — Minister of Labour (Welland): That is not true and you know it!

MR. GREEN: General McNaughton should answer the question.

MR. MCNAUGHTON: No, I will not answer that question in the affirmative.

MR. GREEN: You will not answer the question?

MR. MCNAUGHTON: I will not answer the question in the affirmative. The answer is no.

MR. GREEN: General McNaughton, with regards to the young Canadians in Great Britain who, without any say in the matter, are being remustered into the infantry, perhaps by the thousands, what training will they get before they face the enemy?

MR. MCNAUGHTON: There should be a minimum of six weeks of training for a gunner going on to the infantry.

MR. GREEN: In any event, you are placing a good deal of reliance on the training that these young boys will get when they reach the battalion. What is to happen in the case of a boy going up to the Seaforth Highlanders of Vancouver, as an example, where that unit has been reduced to fifty or a hundred men, and they are in desperate straits to hold their part of the front? What will happen, as you know, will be that that boy will be put right in the line and the chances are that he will be killed or wounded within twenty-four hours!

MR. MCNAUGHTON: If the circumstances of battle permitted, what would happen there is that the unit would be withdrawn.

MR. GREEN: Suppose it is not withdrawn?

MR. MCNAUGHTON: Some of us have been in like position. I have been. When the fate of battle depends on it, it is the duty of every man, regardless of his qualifications, or training, to do the best he can.

MR. GREEN: What does the general think the duty of the men who are in the home defence army fully trained in combat should do?

MR. MCNAUGHTON: He should take up his honourable obligation of service and take it up at once, as other Canadians are doing.

MR. GREEN: Under your present policy, will it be a fact that there will be two types of Canadian soldier: one who fights and one who does not?

MR. MCNAUGHTON: I have the problem of the residual NRMA

personnel in the camps. Even with the most honest searching of our hearts as to how to go about it, we really do not know how to handle it. We have to study and investigate. We have to be sympathetic. We have to be human about it. We will find the answer, although I have not it yet to give you.

ALLAN NEILL (Comox-Alberni): The former minister of national defence (Mr. Ralston), after several visits overseas, comes to the conclusion that he must send overseas these men of the NRMA, and that the situation is urgent. He comes home and so advises the cabinet but he finds his advice ill received. He presses it until he is asked to resign.

What is the position now? The cabinet reverses its policy, in part at least, and decides to send 16,000 men. An order in council is put through today. It was on your advice, Mr. McNaughton, that the government took the steps that were taken in regard to not sending these men overseas which linked you up with the anti-overseas service policy of the government. This afternoon, you reiterated with much force and determination that your full belief is to avoid force or conscription and not one of those men would go over if you could possibly avoid it. Your ideas, your wishes, your views are diametrically opposed to the policy you are now sworn to carry out.

We are now facing the greatest crisis since Confederation. I ask you the question man to man. In your honest opinion, would it not be better for the cabinet to which you now belong, for the Liberal party to which you now adhere, or to the greater interest of the people of Canada whose interests I know you have at heart and the best interests of the war, if you gave way to a man who believes in the policies to be carried out by the government?

MR. KING: This is the first day on which the minister of national defence has ever been on the floor of Parliament. He has a right to expect from hon. members when he comes into this chamber, some due consideration.

KARL HOMUTH (Waterloo South): He asked for it!

MR. KING: Consideration is hardly being shown to the minister when he is asked whether he does not think that he owed it to himself and the government to resign.

MR. NEILL: If the minister does not wish to answer my question he does not have to. But if he is the man I think he is, he will.

JOSEPH NOSEWORTHY (York South): What is the minimum time between the time a man is remustered from the artillery overseas and the time he goes into the action with the infantry?

MR. MCNAUGHTON: Six weeks or more, depending on the ability of the man to pass the tests.

MR. NOSEWORTHY: Wait a minute! That is not the truth!

AN HON. MEMBER: Sit down!

MR. HOMUTH: I am not going to sit down! I rise on a point of order, Mr. Speaker!

AN HON. MEMBER: Where were you in the last war?

MR. HOMUTH: Where were you? All you have been interested in in this House is the baby bonus because you are the biggest man to get it. I want to say to the minister that what he has stated in the House is not according to the evidence that many of us have.

AN HON. MEMBER: Name a case.

MR. HOMUTH: I could name a dozen. Wouldn't you love to have them! What a trimming you would give them!

MR. SPEAKER: Order! The hon. member for Waterloo South will understand that the minister of national defence, although he is not a member of this House yet, is a member of the government and offensive words cannot be said to him. I would ask the hon. member to withdraw that statement.

MR. HOMUTH: Mr. Speaker, in view of the fact that the minister is not a member of the House, actually I do not have to withdraw the statement I made.

SOME HON. MEMBERS: Oh, yes!

MR. HOMUTH: Just you fellows shut up for a minute! You are in a hot spot and you wonder where you are going! I know darned well where you are going! You are going into oblivion!

MR. SPEAKER: Order! I have made a request of the hon. member.

MR. HOMUTH: And I am going to withdraw my remark, Mr. Speaker. ◄

Finally, at 11:20 p.m., the House adjourned. General McNaughton was summoned to return the next day for further questioning. Again, at several points the question and answer session erupted into name-calling.

But the real story lay in Ralston's reaction. Instead of an

aggressive attack on his nemesis, Ralston merely pressed Mc-Naughton on minor technical points. For the greater interest of the nation, the man who could have had the prime minister's desk had passed.

To force Parliament's hand on his administration, Mackenzie King decided to table a motion of confidence. On December 7, 1944, a vote was taken and King secured his vote of confidence by a 143–70 margin. But both Ralston and McNaughton were spent in the controversy. McNaughton twice sought a seat in the House in 1945; once at a February 1945 by-election and again during the 1945 general election. He lost both times and would never try again. Ralston returned to the practice of law in 1945 and died in Montreal three years later.

By the time Germany surrendered on May 8, 1945, only 2,463 Zombies had made it to the front lines.

BLACK FRIDAY
▶▶▶▶▶▶▶▶▶

BLACK FRIDAY was one of the worst days in the history of the Canadian House of Commons: the day the Speaker appeared ready to faint under the pressures of a House in complete chaos; the day the month-long three-way ruckus between the government of Louis St. Laurent and the opposition parties of Conservative leader George Drew and CCF leader Maj. James Coldwell culminated in messy parliamentary anarchy. The rules of order would lay in shambles and the bastion of Canadian democracy would be shaken to its very foundation.

Black Friday was the day of final debate on Bill 298 of the Third Session of the Twenty-second Parliament, an act to establish the Northern Ontario Pipe Line Crown Corporation. While the intentions of the bill were innocent enough, the government's heavy-handedness consolidated the fury of both opposition parties.

Adding fuel to the parliamentary tinderbox in the late spring of 1956 was the political situation in the House. The 1953 general election had reduced the Liberal majority by 20 seats and increased the representation of both the Tories and the CCF, each by 10 seats.

The sponsor of Bill 298, Minister of Trade and Commerce Clarence Decatur Howe, was not a patient man. For Howe, the ideal Parliament was simple, effective and quick, fully compatible with his autocratic manner. The conventional wisdom on Howe was summarized in the House by the Conservative member for Toronto-Greenwood, James Macdonnell: "The minister does not like sharing his powers with Parliament; he does not like sharing his powers with members of his own party, and he has a great aversion even to sharing his powers with the cabinet." It did not help that he was being referred to in the national media as "the most powerful man in Canada." *Time* magazine had even named him Man of the Year.

In the months preceding the pipeline debate, Howe had failed in his attempt to extend his ministerial powers under emergency war legislation, thus suffering his first legislative setback in the House since his entry in 1935. According to Leslie Roberts, Howe's biographer, defeat only served to toughen the minister's attitude to the Commons, as the next round was to prove.

The pipeline debate centred on the creation of a Crown corporation to administer the construction and operation of a trans-Ontario gas pipeline. Albertans had discovered vast surpluses of the natural resource and wanted to sell, east or south. Howe had insisted that the export of gas to the United States was out of the question unless it was first made available to eastern Canadians. Alberta responded that the construction of such a pipeline would delay the flow of profits to Alberta provincial and corporate treasuries. If a $150-million pipeline could be financed, Alberta would export east. A deal was struck with American financiers for a 36-inch pipeline, the largest in the world at the time, to be constructed from Edmonton to Quebec, beginning in 1955. By May of 1956, the start of construction had already been delayed a year and it became apparent that the conglomerate was running out of money. Howe was forced to reorganize federal involvement by creating the Crown corporation to provide the construction conglomerate with sufficient financing so that work could finally begin.

Closure had not been used for 24 years in the House when,

on May 15, Howe invoked it to ram the pipeline bill through first reading on the very day it was introduced. Members reached for their rule books and a flurry of procedural motions were tabled, but to no avail. At 4:30 a.m., the bill received first reading. A week later, under similar duress, the bill was sent to committee of the whole.

Prime Minister St. Laurent personally moved closure on May 31, this time to force the bill out of committee and back before the House for third and final reading. Procedural wrangling had become the norm over the last few weeks. Speaker and Liberal member René Beaudoin was bombarded with requests for rulings.

After the prime minister's motion came a surprise. Colin Cameron, the CCF member for Nanaimo, rose on a question of privilege to quote a letter published in the Ottawa *Journal* by constitutional law expert Eugene Forsey: "The Speaker's words seem to imply that if the rules get seriously in the way of doing something the government very much wants done, no reasonable person can expect the Government to follow them, or the Speaker to enforce them." This letter, declared Cameron, was "an attack on the dignity of Parliament." Cameron moved that Forsey's statement deserved the censure of the House. The Speaker acknowledged that the matter was serious, appearing to agree with Cameron, which could open debate on the matter and tie up the House past St. Laurent's closure deadline. The House adjourned in uncertainty, except in the mind of C.D. Howe. He did not want to further postpone the pipeline.

It did not help that the vehicles of four cabinet members were seen parked in front of the Speaker's residence that evening. The suspicion of collusion was inevitable. For the opposition, the Speaker's decision to entertain Cameron's claim had given rise to hope of breaking Howe.

As the House was called to order at eleven a.m. on Friday morning, June 1, 1956, the leader of the opposition had time to utter but two words before pandemonium broke out.

► **GEORGE DREW** — Leader of the Opposition (Carleton): Mr. Speaker . . .

MR. SPEAKER — Louis-René Beaudoin (Vaudreuil-Solanges): Usually the deputy clerk reads the order, that the Ottawa *Journal* statements of May 31 are deserving of the censure of this House, but I rise at this moment in order to deal with this order.

I have read carefully the articles complained of and I have come to the conclusion that because of the unprecedented circumstances surrounding this pipeline debate, it is impossible, if we are to consider freedom of the press as we should, to take these articles as being breaches of our privileges. I think we should settle our problems ourselves and that those who outside of this House, either in editorial comment or by letters to the editor, write what I consider to be comments which do not go beyond the bounds of fairness, I think they should be allowed. Therefore, I rule the motion made by the hon. member for Nanaimo out of order. Do hon. members want to appeal?

MR. DREW: Are you prepared to hear discussion on that, because . . .

MR. SPEAKER: No.

MR. DREW: . . . we had proceeded with discussion on this motion.

MR. SPEAKER: Whether it is privilege or not, it is my responsibility to decide. Does the hon. gentleman appeal my ruling?

MR. DREW: Mr. Speaker, I appeal your ruling but I also suggest that you should accept this motion.

MR. SPEAKER: The leader of the opposition cannot go beyond appealing my ruling. Call in the members.

AN HON. MEMBER: Dictatorship!

(*And during the calling in of the members:*)

JAMES COLDWELL (Rosetown-Biggar): Mr. Speaker, may I respectfully draw to your attention that you directed the hon. member for Nanaimo to make that motion.

MR. SPEAKER: There cannot be any debate at this moment. The bells are ringing and members are being called in.

MR. DREW: Mr. Speaker, the rights of Parliament are more important than bells. You drafted this motion, Mr. Speaker. You accepted the motion and the motion is now in possession of the House and you have no right to hear anything that interferes with the discussion. I protest against your ruling.

SOME HON. MEMBERS: Sit down.

ALFRED ELLIS (Regina City): Keep quiet over there.

ALISTAIR STEWART (Winnipeg North): Why don't you throw away the mace?

JOHN DIEFENBAKER (Lake Centre): Why did you change overnight? Are you afraid today?

WILLIAM ROWE :(Dufferin-Simcoe): What took place in the dark? ◄

Drew's appeal of the Speaker's decision on Cameron's motion was defeated 140–51. Members catcalled throughout the vote and the fight continued no sooner was the Speaker's ruling declared sustained. It worsened when Speaker Beaudoin continued with his surprises.

► **STANLEY KNOWLES** (Winnipeg North Centre): Mr. Speaker, I move, seconded by the hon. member for Saskatoon (Mr. Knight) that the House do now adjourn. It should read that the House be dissolved.

DONALD FLEMING (Eglinton): Leave the matter to the people.

MR. SPEAKER: It is obvious that in this House there are feelings that are perhaps extraordinary. I think there is perhaps on the part of some hon. members what I may term anger.

MR. DREW: There is!

MR. SPEAKER: I want to tell hon. members that I know what my responsibilities are and I am fully conscious of every step that I am taking. I am prepared to take the responsibility before this House and the country for what I do. Hon. members know that it is within my jurisdiction — indeed it is my duty — to make a ruling whenever I consider that I must make one.

These days are not easy ones. Today we meet; I make a ruling.

MR. FLEMING: Without hearing any argument?

MR. SPEAKER: That it should be met with criticism, or even with sincere feelings, perhaps of indignation, is the privilege of hon. members. But the ruling on appeal was submitted to the House. Now the hon. member from Winnipeg North Centre is moving that the House do now adjourn. I consider, and I have thought very seriously about this, that yesterday around 5:15, I made a very serious mistake in allowing the point of order, and I feel the House should not suffer any prejudice on my account. The rules of the House are devised to protect the minorities. Yes, they are. But I will add the counterpart to that. The rules of this House are devised to protect the minorities against the oppression of the majority and the majority against obstruction by the minority. I submit to the House that, in my view, the House should revert to the position where it was yesterday when I was brought back to the chair at 5:15. Those in favour of supporting the Speaker's ruling please say yea.

MAJOR COLDWELL: What are you doing, Mr. Speaker?

MR. DREW: On a question of privilege, Mr. Speaker . . .

SOME HON. MEMBERS: Sit down.

MR. DREW: . . . I move, seconded by the hon. member for Dufferin-Simcoe (Mr. Rowe) that in view of the unprecedented action of Mr. Speaker in improperly reversing his own decision without notice and without giving any opportunity for discussion, this House resolves that it no longer has any confidence in its presiding officer.

MR. SPEAKER: The leader of the opposition understands, of course, that this is a motion that must go on the order paper and receive 48 hours' notice.

MR. KNOWLES: Mr. Speaker, on the point of order, there is a lot of heat around here and I am absorbing some of it. Whatever you may feel about any mistakes you made yesterday, the fact is that this is a new day and we are now on the order for motions. We cannot jump from motions to the position in which we found ourselves yesterday at five o'clock, without first reaching the orders of the day. In the meantime, there is before the House a motion duly made and duly seconded, namely to adjourn the House. It is my privilege to appeal your ruling if you so rule.

MR. SPEAKER: I will say this to the hon. member. I will agree with him that his motion was made before I indicated my position, and I will allow his appeal and submit it to the House. ◄

Knowles's appeal was defeated 143–51. Question Period ensued, and immediately after it Speaker Beaudoin again introduced his proposed course of action, to revert the House to the point in time before his "mistake" of the previous evening. The Speaker called for a vote.

► **MR. SPEAKER:** In my opinion, the yeas have it. Call in the members.

MR. DREW: Mr. Speaker —

MR. FLEMING: Mr. Speaker —

DAVIE FULTON (Kamloops): Mr. Speaker —

MR. KNOWLES: Mr. Speaker —

SOME HON. MEMBERS: Hail, hail, the gang's all there!

MR. DREW: Mr. Speaker, do I understand that you will do nothing?

MR. DIEFENBAKER: Has the prime minister no control over his followers?

MR. COLDWELL: Mr. Speaker, are you not going to call order?

MR. SPEAKER: There is nothing before the House at the moment.

MR. KNOWLES: There is no House.

MR. COLDWELL: Mr. Speaker, I protest against this. Parliament has ceased to function.

MR. DIEFENBAKER: Where is the prime minister?

MR. ROWE: Is he afraid to dissolve Parliament? Why not do it yourself? You are doing everything else yourself.

PAUL MARTIN — Minister of National Health and Welfare (Essex East): You have delayed things for three weeks. You led it too! Don't say a word!

MR. FLEMING: Mr. Speaker, it should be put on the record that when an hon. member rose on a question of privilege you sat down and refused to hear him and the Liberals instigated such an outburst of disorder that no one could be heard. This is the lowest moment in Canadian parliamentary history! There has never been anything like it!

LESTER PEARSON — Secretary of State for External Affairs (Algoma East): I thought that was last night.

THOMAS MILLER BELL (Saint John-Albert): This is black Friday, boy.

JEAN LESAGE — Minister of Northern Affairs and National Resources (Montmagny-L'Islet): You brought it on! You did it yourself!

MR. FLEMING: How absurd can you get?

MR. MARTIN: The minority is not running this Parliament.

CLAYTON HODGSON (Victoria, Ontario): Hitlerism!

SOME HON. MEMBERS:

There will always be a pipe line.

The pipe line shall be free.

The gas shall flow from west to east in each locality.

There shall always be a pipe line.

The pipe line shall be free.

MR. FLEMING: Not Parliament.

SOME HON. MEMBERS:
For Fulton means no more to you than Fulton means to me.
There'll always be a pipe line.
The pipe line shall be free.
MR. FLEMING: Free to American investors.
SOME HON. MEMBERS:
I've been working on the pipe line, all the day through,
I've been working on the pipe line, just to make the Tories blue.
Can't you hear the Tories moaning, getting up so early in the morn';
Hear the CCF'ers groaning, for the pipe line's getting warm.
MR. ROWE: He who laughs best who laughs last. Go to the country and find out. ◄

The vote was taken on Speaker Beaudoin's proposed course of action and accepted 142–0, both opposition parties refusing to vote. Immediately after lunch the Speaker secured a motion to revert the House back to May 31, to continue consideration of Bill 298 in committee of the whole. The deputy chairman took the chair and his authority was immediately challenged, this time by David Fulton. Yet another vote was taken and again defeated 144–49. Knowles then challenged the authority of the chairman of the committee of the whole. A fifth and sixth vote were taken and the House finally returned to committee of the whole. Ten hours later, at 1:47 a.m., the House adjourned, but not before Mr. Coldwell got in a final comment.

► **MR. COLDWELL:** Mr. Speaker, the people in the galleries have seen a farce tonight.
JAMES MCCANN — Minister of National Revenue (Renfrew South): You are the farce.
MR. COLDWELL: This is the worst proceeding that has ever been seen in this Parliament. ◄

On June 6, the day the Senate approved the pipeline bill, Drew rose in the House and formally tabled an extraordinary motion of non-confidence against the Speaker. Thirty minutes later, just as he was walking towards his seat in the House, the Liberal member for Vancouver-Burrard, Jack MacDougall, suffered a fatal heart attack. The House immediately adjourned.

Although Drew's motion was later defeated, Speaker Beaudoin was completely discredited and would soon resign, never again to seek election to the House of Commons. Most political commentators point to the arrogance of the Liberal government during the pipeline debate, especially the frequent recourse to closure, as the single most important reason why, after 22 uninterrupted years in power, they won fewer seats than Diefenbaker's Progressive Conservative candidates in the next three federal elections.

FOOT IN THE MOUTH
►►►►►►►►►►►►►►

WHEN THE POLLS CLOSED on the June 10, 1957, federal election, the Conservatives had been elected to 112 seats compared with 105 for the Liberals. With 48 members from other parties such as the CCF or Social Credit, Louis St. Laurent could name a cabinet, preside over the opening of Parliament and risk an eventual defeat on a non-confidence vote. For a full week, the 75-year-old prime minister pondered his options. On June 17, he announced his decision to resign. Four days later, John Diefenbaker was sworn in as the thirteenth prime minister of Canada, at the head of a minority Conservative government. Two and a half months later, St. Laurent announced that he was stepping down as leader of the Liberal party.

A leadership convention was scheduled for January 14–16, 1958, in Ottawa. Any race that might have been, ended when candidate Lester Pearson, the former minister for external affairs, was awarded the Nobel Peace Prize on December 10, 1957, for his diplomatic efforts during the Suez Canal crisis. At the Liberal convention, Pearson beat the only other candidate, Paul Martin, Sr., by a 1,084–305 margin.

In the House of Commons on January 20, 1958, Diefenbaker paid tribute to the outgoing leader of the Liberal party. St. Laurent, now mere opposition critic on federal-provincial relations, acknowledged Diefenbaker's generous words. The new leader of the opposition, Lester B. Pearson, spoke briefly and then the Commons returned to regular business. Immediately after Question Period, Pearson made the biggest blunder of his political career.

► **LESTER B. PEARSON** — Leader of the Opposition (Algoma East): Mr. Speaker, it is my duty, of course, to point out whenever I can and to drive home as vigorously as I can, the inadequacy of government measures, the sins of omission and commission of the government in the handling of current problems.

Mr. Speaker, it looks more and more as if the government has really shot its bolt with the increases in social security and veterans benefits, cash advances on farm-stored grain, increased housing loans and the disappointing tax reductions from our surplus which fell so very far short of their pre-election promises. That, Mr. Speaker, is the record of Tory achievement in seven months, plus the appointment of sundry royal commissions and missions which for the time being will help some chickens from coming home to roost on the limb on which the government has got itself by its promises.

In view of the desirability at this time of having a government pledged to implementation of Liberal policies of the kind outlined in the resolutions of the national Liberal convention . . .

DOUGLAS HARKNESS — Minister of Agriculture (Calgary North): What are these Liberal policies? Nobody has heard of them in this country for 40 years!

MR. PEARSON: Mr. Speaker, it is our view that His Excellency's advisers should, in the interest of this House of Commons, submit their resignations. I confess, Mr. Speaker, that an election at this time, in the winter months . . .

GEORGE HEES — Minister of Transport (Toronto-Broadview): We'd beat the pants off you!

DONALD FLEMING — Minister of Finance (Eglinton): Mike, it is sad to see you come to this.

MR. PEARSON: This Parliament is only seven months old. We would be a minority of members, it is true, but so are they. And we represent nearly a quarter of a million more voters. This Parliament has a perfect right to give its confidence to a new government. I would be prepared, if called upon, to form such a government to tackle immediately the formidable problem of ending the Tory pause and getting this country back on the Liberal highway of progress. I therefore move, seconded by the hon. member for Quebec East (Mr. St. Laurent): His Excellency's advisers should, in the opinion of this House, submit their resignation forthwith. ◄

In his memoirs, Donald Fleming called Pearson's motion a "hare-brained manoeuvre. He did not wish an election. He did not wish us to dissolve Parliament. He simply wanted us to give up our places on the Treasury benches!" The Liberal government had resigned but six months earlier. Diefenbaker had barely begun to implement a legislative program when the apprentice opposition leader asked for his resignation.

Diefenbaker rose and delivered a deadly rebuke, reminding Pearson that since the June 1957 election, the Tories had won both by-elections. "Across the way, Mr. Speaker, sit the purveyors of doom," gloated Diefenbaker. "My friends, you could not delude the people of Canada last June. Whenever the election comes, I am sure they will not be deluded by that type of argument."

Pearson had seriously jeopardized the political chances of his party and was now at the mercy of the Diefenbaker minority government. The Chief dissolved Parliament 10 days later. Canadians returned the Conservatives with what was then the largest majority in Canadian history, with 208 Conservative members elected to the 265-seat House of Commons. The Liberals dropped from 105 to 49 members.

Towards the end of that January day in the Commons, as Pearson sat in a self-described "state of some depression," a backbencher approached his dejected leader. "That was a magnificent speech, Mr. Pearson. Too bad you didn't stop before you ended it."

9
Patriotism Revisited
▶▶▶▶▶▶▶▶▶▶▶▶▶▶▶▶▶▶▶▶▶▶▶▶▶▶▶▶

PERSONAL ENMITY
▶▶▶▶▶▶▶▶▶▶▶▶

THE PRIME MINISTER OF CANADA AND THE LEADER of the official opposition usually maintain cordial relations. Aside from the expected give and take on the floor of the House, or the exchange of political rhetoric with the media, the federal leaders have only rarely shown genuine dislike for each other. But it had happened between King and Meighen in the 1920s and it would happen again on October 2, 1962.

Wounded by a financial crisis smack in the middle of the 1962 election campaign, Prime Minister John Diefenbaker was returned to the House with only 116 members. The Liberal party had 99 members elected. The Social Credit party, an element in federal politics since 1935, had been reduced to a provincial caucus, with 26 of its 30 members elected in the 1962 election coming from Quebec ridings. The CCF had been reorganized as the New Democratic Party in August 1961 and managed to elect 19 members to the short-lived Twenty-fifth Parliament.

When the House convened, the Liberal leader of the opposition, Lester Pearson, moved a non-confidence motion the moment the throne speech was seconded. Immediately, Diefenbaker stood. Throughout his response, he was taunted by the Liberal opposition. Diefenbaker took it personally and then, so did Pearson.

▶ **RIGHT HON. JOHN DIEFENBAKER** — Prime Minister (Prince Albert): Mr. Speaker, in order to deal with some of the statements that have been made by the leader of the opposition in the last few months, I am going to say to him at once that I am not going to put these statements on Hansard, these personal attacks. I could answer them, but I am not going to get down in the gutter with the leader of the opposition.

LESTER PEARSON — Leader of the Opposition (Algoma East): That is where you have been for years!

MR. DIEFENBAKER: It has been a concerted effort on the part of the Liberal party and was declared to be such by one of them. It was stated that everything would be done in order to personally attack me.

Criticism is essential in the democratic process, but the organized deluge of defamation and adjectival abuse that has been heaped upon the government of this country and myself as leader has never been equalled in the history of Canada.

I am going to place the record here! Yesterday, as I listened to the leader of the opposition, I had to compliment him for his restraint in not saying inside the House, when he is face to face, what he said outside. Never before has there been the equal in vehemence and virulence displayed in the public affairs in this country.

I realize that in the heat of debate we often say things about one another we wish we had not said. But, sir, when speeches are prepared in advance and handed out by the leader of the opposition, I say to him . . .

MR. PEARSON: Put them on the record!

MR. DIEFENBAKER: I am not going to spoil the record with that!

MR. PEARSON: What a phoney attitude! Repeat them! Put them on the record!

MR. DIEFENBAKER: Mr. Speaker, it is obvious that I have touched a tender spot. They show a disregard for the political amenities of political controversy.

MR. PEARSON: Mr. Speaker, on a point of order, the prime minister has accused me of making a personal statement of criticism and vilification, and using other adjectives in connection with these statements made outside the House. I ask the prime minister to substantiate that allegation by putting this statement on the record inside the House.

MR. DIEFENBAKER: Mr. Speaker, I am too old for that. When defamation takes place, do you repeat the defamation against yourself?

MR. PEARSON: Put up or shut up!

MR. DIEFENBAKER: Mr. Speaker, I must be irritating some parts of the anatomy of the opposition. I do not mind criticism. But, Sir, all through the campaign there was ridicule poured on the fact that I have not an Anglo-Saxon name. Their advertising used the first two syllables of my name in ridicule. I finally found where they got my dog Happy into it! That was about the last touch! ◄

This time, Pearson had played his cards right. John Diefenbaker was a hunted man. Revolt was brewing in his cabinet. He and his Conservative party would soon be in opposition, but not until a grave international crisis terrified the country.

THE CUBAN MISSILE CRISIS
►►►►►►►►►►►►►►►►

T HE WORLD HAD NEVER come so close to nuclear war as it did in the latter weeks of October 1962. At 4 a.m. on October 22, 1962, a diplomatic request was received from the United States that refuelling privileges of Cuban and Czechoslovakian flights at Gander, Newfoundland, be temporarily suspended. Diefenbaker was then advised that the former American ambassador to Canada, Livingston Merchant, had requested to meet with him at 5 p.m. When Merchant arrived at Diefenbaker's East Block office, he brought with him photographic evidence of the buildup of Soviet nuclear weapons in Cuba: ballistic missiles, some with a range of 22,000 miles. The Americans would be implementing a naval blockade of Cuba, Merchant informed the prime minister. He then asked Diefenbaker to place the Canadian component of the North American Air Defence Agreement (NORAD) at full alert.

The prime minister was miffed at receiving this information from an emissary. He picked up his phone and called the American president, John F. Kennedy. Kennedy explained the international subtleties of a coordinated response to the continental military threat. In his memoirs, Diefenbaker recalls stating to Kennedy: "Our defences were alerted and would be ready if a real crisis developed but that I did not believe that Mr. Khrushchev would allow things to reach that stage." Minutes later, Kennedy went on television and informed a shocked world of the Soviet activities. Shortly after, the leader of the opposition called Diefenbaker and suggested that he make a statement to the House.

► **RIGHT HON. JOHN DIEFENBAKER** — Prime Minister (Prince Albert): Mr. Speaker, the President pointed out that on the island of Cuba preparations were being made for the construction of bases for the launching of offensive weapons in the form of I.R.B.M.s, and that this constitutes a threat to most of the cities of North America including our major cities in Canada. It is a time when each of us must endeavour to do his part to assure the preservation of peace not only in this hemisphere but everywhere in the world. Our duty, as I see it, is not to fan the flames of fear but to do our part to bring about relief from the great tensions of the hour. ◄

When Diefenbaker retired from the chamber, he was told that American NORAD forces had been elevated to Defcon 3. (The NORAD scale of defence conditions ranged from Defcon 5 — normal — to Defcon 0 — nuclear attack. Defcon 3 indicated "imminent danger.") The minister of national defence, Doug Harkness, requested from the prime minister the permission to authorize a similar upgrade of Canadian forces. But Diefenbaker refused, requesting instead that the request be placed before the cabinet, set to meet the next morning. Meanwhile, American vessels rushed to close the line around the island of Cuba as 18 Soviet ships and six submarines continued their voyage across the Atlantic.

At the Tuesday, October 23, cabinet meeting, Diefenbaker argued strongly against the upgrade, and the meeting adjourned without any decision. Harkness quietly told his military advisers to go ahead with the full-alert status except the recall of men on leave. Ships left port and airports were provisioned. At 2:23 p.m., Question Period began. Harkness was hoping he would not be asked any questions.

► **PAUL HELLYER** (Trinity): I should like to direct a question to the minister of national defence. With respect to the crisis, have any direct steps been taken by the Canadian government, other than the withdrawing of landing and transit facilities for Soviet aircraft? For example, have Canadian units assigned to NORAD been alerted and have any special orders been transmitted to naval units in the north Atlantic?

DOUGLAS HARKNESS — Minister of National Defence (Calgary North): Mr. Speaker, by and large the answer to that question is no. Naturally, we have been reviewing plans to meet all possible contingencies.◄

Events were moving rapidly. In Washington, President Kennedy was well engaged in his game of brinkmanship with Khrushchev. The Soviet fleet was approaching the 800-mile blockade line established by the U.S. Navy. On Tuesday night, Kennedy moved the line back to 500 miles and released to the media the satellite pictures of the Soviet missile bases. At 10 a.m., October 24, the first of the Russian vessels approached the line and stopped, dead in the water. Some Soviet vessels veered off course. Another allowed an American search. Its cargo hold contained only petroleum and it was allowed through. Cabinet met, and again Harkness pleaded for authority to upgrade the Canadian military. "Harkness and three-quarters of the cabinet [were] now demanding the increased NORAD alert," wrote Knowlton Nash in his book *Kennedy and Diefenbaker*. "However, Diefenbaker and [external affairs minister Howard] Green vociferously opposed the move." Again, the meeting broke up without any decision. When Question Period began, the House was not long in sensing the indecisiveness.

► **MR. HELLYER:** I wish to direct a question to the minister of national defence. Is it a fact that Canada has defaulted on its solemn obligation in respect of the NORAD treaty, in time of crisis, by refusing to accede to the request of the United States air force to arm Canadian Bomarc squadrons with atomic warheads and to permit United States airplanes to use Canadian air bases?

MR. HARKNESS: Mr. Speaker, the answer is emphatically no. We have not defaulted. ◄

Some American forces were elevated to Defcon 2, which meant that an enemy attack was expected. Harkness pleaded with Diefenbaker, who finally conceded. The country was informed the next day as Diefenbaker informed the House that "the Canadian component of the NORAD forces has been placed upon the same level of readiness as the United States forces." In fact, Diefenbaker had suddenly and inexplicably become much more sympathetic to the American predicament. He added in the House that "there is a debate regarding the legality of the quarantine. Legalistic arguments cannot erase the fact that the Soviet Union has posed a new and immediate threat to the security not only of the United States but of Canada as well. It is the Soviet Union which has disturbed the balance. It is for it and Cuba to restore that balance."

An exchange of diplomatic letters had begun between Moscow and Washington when, suddenly, an American spy plane was shot down over Cuba on Saturday morning, October 27. American military officers pressed the American president for authority to invade Cuba immediately. On Saturday night,

Kennedy told the Soviet ambassador that unless Khrushchev agreed to a deal by Tuesday, Cuba would be invaded.

The world braced itself for nuclear war. Howard Green, secretary of state for external affairs, later told the House of Commons, "I believed that before morning Ottawa might be demolished as well as Montreal, Toronto and Vancouver." His fears were shared by Canadians from coast to coast. But at 9 a.m. on Sunday, Khrushchev's reply to Kennedy's ultimatum was broadcast in Moscow. The terms had been accepted; the crisis was over. The missile bases would be dismantled, the blockade lifted, and there would be no invasion of Cuba.

Diefenbaker had shown an extraordinary ability for vacillation and had missed an excellent opportunity to raise his political stock. "It profoundly undermined the prime minister's political support in Canada as a significantly increasing number of Canadians felt Diefenbaker had inexcusably dithered or worse in the Cuban Missile Crisis," concluded Knowlton Nash. Within six months, John Diefenbaker's Conservatives would be in opposition and would remain there for 16 years.

A FLAG IS BORN
▶▶▶▶▶▶▶▶▶▶

JOHN DIEFENBAKER had been in opposition for almost two years when Lester B. Pearson introduced the notion of a new, distinctive Canadian flag. On May 14, 1963, Pearson had revealed his proposal for a new flag, with a design composed of "a white field charged with three maple leaves conjoined on a single stem." Diefenbaker wrapped the Union Jack around himself and his supporters, declaring the Red Ensign as an absolute untouchable of Canadian society.

The Red Ensign was a red flag with the Union Jack in one corner and the coat of arms of Canada in another. It had become the accepted flag of Canada. But the Union Jack was the flag of the United Kingdom, with which Canada, since the Statute of Westminster in 1931, shared little but language and a monarch.

Faithful to the second component of the nomenclature of his political party, Diefenbaker would have nothing to do with a new flag. He rose in the House and shook his finger at Pearson, warning that Canadians would have his political skin if he pursued this crazy concept of a maple leaf flag. At first, his Progressive Conservative caucus bought it. Pearson served notice of his motion for a new flag on May 28, 1964, and the chase was on.

On June 1, the Conservative member for Elgin, James McBain, responded with a resolution to retain the Red Ensign as Canada's national flag. For the next six and a half months, the Conservative filibuster on the flag debate would irk, tire and then, finally, outrage many Canadians. Pearson would win this one by sheer patience.

Some opposition interventions, designed not to convince but rather to occupy time, bordered on the ridiculous. To wit, these August 12 and August 17 Conservative contributions:

► **GORDON CLANCY** (Yorkton): Mr. Speaker, I cannot understand the way in which the government introduced the flag resolution. I think it is a political gimmick. We have a great deal more business to do in the country. And I say that this House as a whole, including myself, is receiving a very bad black eye from the public. They say "what are you wasting your time about?"

If the people of this country want a new flag then let us find out what they want. Are we to sell all our traditions? I have read the history books and let me tell you that Wolfe won the battle on the plains of Abraham by a fluke; Montcalm lost it because he was asleep, and that is a fact!

FREDERICK BIGG (Athabasca): Mr. Speaker, they took Joan of Arc's flag down. They put her lily banner in the dirt and she was only a woman. But what a glorious woman she was! She put her lily banner out in front and never looked back, and with her very small army swept the ranks clear. She put the rightful heir, I am led to believe, on the throne of France. Then the king of France ratted on her, and you know the rest. Now she is a saint. Which of those opposite in their male pride will stand up and say that they think the lily banner of France or the cross of St. George should be laid in the dirt? ◄

Historians were not kind to the Tory leader and his troops. "Silly byplay," wrote Peter Newman. Charles Lynch added that "the flag debate may be the stuff of which history is made. But if it is, the historians are going to be bored stiff."

And then, suddenly, the flag debate became interesting. On September 10, Pearson invited Diefenbaker, NDP leader Tommy Douglas and the leader of the Social Credit Party,

Robert Thompson, to his office where a deal was hammered out. A 15-member committee was created to report to the House in six weeks, a brief reprieve. Then, *dame chance* came to Pearson's assistance. As the committee wound up its work, a misunderstanding by the five Conservative members produced a unanimous vote on one of the design recommendations for a new flag, which has since become the national flag.

Diefenbaker denounced the committee's recommendation, but the days of his party's filibuster were numbered. Conservative caucus members began breaking ranks with the Chief. On December 9, Diefenbaker's Quebec lieutenant himself, Léon Balcer (Trois-Rivières), rose on a question of privilege. "Mr. Speaker, for months the House has been witnessing an unparalleled debate which is completely paralysing the business of this House, where it is impossible to reach any decision whatsoever," he protested. "I invite the prime minister to give notice that he will have this question settled by applying the rule of closure." The Liberal government was only too happy to oblige.

At 1:20 a.m., December 15, 1964, the Speaker announced over loud protests from the Conservative opposition that the prime minister would have 20 minutes to speak, after which the House would vote on the flag committee report. Pearson, amidst heavy opposition heckling, weathered the storm and delivered his flag.

► **RIGHT HON. LESTER B. PEARSON** — Prime Minister (Algoma East): Mr. Speaker, I should like to begin by calling attention to the fact that this debate has seen 270, plus, speeches in the House, 190, plus, of which have come from the official opposition.

RIGHT HON. JOHN DIEFENBAKER — Leader of the Opposition (Prince Albert): And we successfully changed the thinking of the government on the first flag.

MR. PEARSON: I wonder if my hon. friend could contain himself for about 20 minutes. Mr. Speaker, if the House wishes to give unanimous consent, I would be very glad indeed to take only half of that time and give the last ten minutes to the leader of the opposition if he would like to have them.

MR. DIEFENBAKER: Mr. Speaker, when the Greeks produce gifts, we recognize what they mean. The prime minister is throttling Parliament and is tearing down the flag which has flown over this country for 100 years. He is trying to be facetious at a time like this.

MR. PEARSON: Mr. Speaker, perhaps I should have learned from experience that offers of cooperation to that quarter usually do not get a very friendly reception.

This debate has gone on for a long time. In order to preserve to Parliament the right of decision, it was necessary to invoke a rule which I hope will only be very rarely invoked in this Parliament, the rule of closure. Otherwise, we would have made a farce of parliamentary debate on this matter. The motion of the government [for closure] was sustained, Mr. Speaker, by representatives of every party in the House, including the deputy leader of the Conservative party.

Now, Mr. Speaker, we are approaching the end of a long, hard and sincere fight by hon. members opposite for what they considered to be the national flag for Canada. I have never denied them that right, nor have I ever denied the sincerity with which they made the fight.

MR. DIEFENBAKER: The right hon. gentleman has done everything to divide this country.

MR. PEARSON: Will the right hon. gentleman contain himself for two or three minutes longer, and then we will vote.

MR. DIEFENBAKER: When the right hon. gentleman starts giving me advice, I say to him, you have done more to divide Canada than any other prime minister.

MR. PEARSON: I think we should be sympathetic to the right hon. gentleman because he is feeling the frustrations of failure.

AN HON. MEMBER: Shut up and sit down!

MR. DIEFENBAKER: I challenge the minister of national health and welfare [Judy LaMarsh] because she was the one who said, with exquisite femininity, "shut up and sit down." I say to the prime minister, is he experiencing the happiness of having throttled discussion in Parliament? Is that what he is experiencing at this time when a flag is being born?

MR. PEARSON: Before I was interrupted by the right hon. gentleman, that master of parliamentary procedure, I was trying to say that this is a good flag, Canada's flag; the red maple leaf flag. Why cannot my right hon. friend forget the passions, the prejudices and the bitterness of the fights of the past few months and rally behind this Canadian flag and make it the emblem of unity in this country? Why can he not do this?

MR. DIEFENBAKER: A flag by closure; imposed by closure.

MR. PEARSON: All right, Mr. Speaker, there is no use making an appeal, that is obvious. I regret very much that a man who has attained such prominence in the public life of Canada for so many years would take this attitude at the end of this debate on a matter of this national importance.

I make one final suggestion, Mr. Speaker, and that is that if this motion carries — and it is going to carry — surely hon. gentlemen opposite do not wish to be put on the record as voting against a design which is going to be our national flag.

JAY MONTEITH (Perth): Oh, nuts! Don't be crazy! I am going to be recorded!

MR. PEARSON: I make this appeal to them. They can turn it down with insult and contumely if they so desire. On this side of the House, there are Canadians as loyal to the past as any hon. gentlemen opposite, and they will vote for the flag. We on this side, and a good many on the other side of the House will vote with pride and confidence. ◄

Then the Speaker rose and called for the yeas and the nays. Pearson watched as opposition members rose to force a recorded vote, ignoring his last-minute plea. The members were called in for the vote on the new flag, which was tallied just after 2 a.m. The design we know today was resolved 163–78 as Canada's national flag amidst boisterous renditions of "O Canada" and "God Save the Queen."

THE MAD BOMBER OF PARLIAMENT HILL
▶▶▶▶▶▶▶▶▶▶▶▶▶▶▶▶▶▶▶▶▶▶▶▶▶

"**MR. SPEAKER, GENTLEMEN,** I might as well give you a blast to wake you up. For one whole year I have thought of nothing but how to exterminate as many of you as possible. The only bills you pass are the ones that line your pockets. I move that we elect a president right now. All in favour, raise your right hand. If not in favour, God help you."

Ottawa police found this speech in the tattered, blood-stained coat pocket of Paul Joseph Chartier. Later dubbed the "the mad bomber of Parliament Hill" by the press, Chartier had naively written to the clerk for permission to address the House of Commons. It was denied.

Determined and demented, the 45-year-old Chartier entered Centre Block on May 18, 1966, concealing five sticks of dynamite. Outside the public gallery on the south side, he asked the guards where the washrooms were. He then inquired whether they would save him a seat. When they refused he mused aloud, "I'll just have to take my chances," and made his way to the men's washroom.

In the House, John Nicholson, minister of labour and member for Vancouver Centre, began to respond to a motion from Frank Howard, the NDP member for Skeena. Howard wanted copies of any correspondence in the minister's possession with regards to the Seafarers International Union. Nicholson began to explain that such papers were confidential.

"I presume that technically the hon. member may be entitled to communications between other organizations . . ."

Up one floor, in the men's washroom, Chartier unwrapped his lethal package and lit the fuse, intent on throwing it upon the floor of the House of Commons. He turned slowly and began his walk towards the public gallery. But as soon as he pushed the swing door of the washroom stall, the bomb exploded, killing him instantly. A tremendous blast reverberated throughout the chamber. Nicholson stopped speaking. At first members thought that the noise came from some backbencher antic in the private members' lobby. Confusion reigned for several moments. The Hansard excerpt contains the italicized editor's note: "At this point a loud explosion was heard in the chamber." None of the members were yet aware how close the Parliament of Canada had come to the agony of a horrible national tragedy.

Nicholson tried to continue but rampant rumours and louder and louder muttering around him made it obvious that continuing the business of the House was impossible. The Speaker recognized the senior member to his left.

▶ **RIGHT HON. JOHN DIEFENBAKER** — Leader of the Opposition (Prince Albert): Mr. Speaker, the reason for the conversation in the chamber is the current report that someone has just passed away within the precincts of the House of Commons. I suggest to the prime minister, and I do so in the desire that the House should not be carrying on under such circumstances, that it might be worth considering that this House should adjourn.

RIGHT HON. LESTER B. PEARSON — Prime Minister (Algoma East): It appears that there was a bomb explosion in the washroom at this end of the third floor and that a man has been killed, under circumstances which are not quite clear. There has been a good deal of damage done to the washroom and a certain amount of confusion is natural. Perhaps my right hon. friend's suggestion should be adopted and the House could adjourn until four o'clock, when the situation will be cleared up and we can resume. ◀

The House adjourned for an hour. At 4 p.m., debate began anew as if nothing had happened. Twice, in the first minutes of resumed debate, Speaker Lucien Lamoureux was on his feet. "Order, please! That kind of question cannot be accepted," he reprimanded the first orator. The House was back to normal, the mad bomber but a mystery for Ottawa police.

VIVE LE QUEBEC LIBRE!
▶▶▶▶▶▶▶▶▶▶▶▶▶▶

LESTER B. PEARSON HAD been prime minister for four and a half years, and before that leader of the opposition for five years. However, it would be his nine-year tenure as secretary of state for external affairs that would carry him through the difficult days of the visit of the president of France in 1967.

Charles de Gaulle had come to visit the world exposition being held in Montreal. The House of Commons was in the midst of a summer recess when the president's yacht anchored at Quebec City on July 23. Pearson remained in Ottawa and did not greet the president, to protest the French president's decision to visit Quebec City before Ottawa. After a number of events in the provincial capital, de Gaulle's cavalcade made its way slowly down the north shore highway to Montreal. At

Montreal's City Hall, de Gaulle offered historic words to an enthusiastic crowd estimated at 15,000.

"Ce soir, ici, et tout le long de ma route, je me suis trouvé dans une atmosphère du même genre que celle de la Libération! Vive Montréal! Vive le Québec! Vive le Québec libre! Vive le Canada français! Vive la France!"

There were no disavowals of the rebellious remarks by officials of the Quebec government, amongst them Marcel Masse, minister of state for education and minister responsible for receiving foreign heads of state. Pearson was at 24 Sussex Drive and had watched de Gaulle utter "Vive le Québec libre!" on television. Two emergency cabinet meetings were held the next day. Some ministers called for an immediate severing of diplomatic relations with France. Pearson chose a softer approach. He went on national television.

"Certain statements by the president," he said, "are unacceptable to the Canadian people." The next morning, de Gaulle's press aides announced that the French president had cancelled his Ottawa visit. He was on the next plane to Paris.

When the House reconvened in late September, there was little comment on the de Gaulle fiasco. But the French president had not finished meddling.

Back in Paris, de Gaulle instructed his ministers to secretly negotiate directly with Quebec. On November 26, de Gaulle called a press conference to announce a comprehensive agreement between the French republic and the Canadian province. He then added that Quebec's independence was inevitable. "Il faut que la France soit la France," he concluded. De Gaulle's remarks were brought to Pearson's attention just as he was boarding a plane in London, England, bound for Ottawa. The next day his response received the unanimous approval of the leaders of all opposition parties.

► **RIGHT HON. LESTER B. PEARSON** — Prime Minister (Algoma East): Mr. Speaker, I said in my statement of July 25 that Canada has always had a special relationship with France, which is the Motherland to so many of her citizens. I should like to confirm those words today.

General de Gaulle's statements will obviously arouse discord in

Canada. I am sure the people of this country will be restrained in their response to it, as I am in mine today, so as not to serve the purpose of those who would disunite and divide our country. Indeed, Mr. Speaker, it is intolerable that a head of a foreign state or government should recommend a course of political or constitutional action which would destroy Canadian confederation and the unity of the Canadian state. The future of Canada, Mr. Speaker, will be decided in Canada, by Canadians!

To those who would set us free, we answer, "we are free!"

To those who would disunite us, we answer, "we remain united!"

On April 19, 1960, the head of another state, speaking in Ottawa had this to say. I quote from his speech: "How do Canadians appear to us? Politically, a state which has found the means to unite two societies very different in origin, language and religion, forging a national character even though spread out over three thousand miles; a solid and stable state."

Mr. Speaker, I agree with the words of General de Gaulle in 1960. I disagree with his words in November 1967. ◄

SHOTGUN CALL
▶▶▶▶▶▶▶▶▶▶

FROM THE MOMENT he was announced as the fourth ballot winner of the leadership of the Liberal party, Pierre Trudeau was hounded by the media for a statement on his intentions with regards to Parliament. Journalists kept a constant vigil on his every move and on all entrances into Rideau Hall, the Governor General's residence. Trudeau would need Governor General Roland Michener's signature to dissolve Parliament and call a general election.

On April 23, 1968, the new prime minister slipped out of his West Block office by a secret stairway and escaped in an unmarked car. Arriving at the Governor General's residence, Trudeau scaled the fence to avoid the watchful eye of the press. There he secured the necessary signature for a dissolution. Only his closest advisers knew of his intentions.

With no reported sightings at the Governor General's residence, members filed into the House for daily business. Opposition leaders had on their desks speeches of tribute to Lester

Pearson and congratulations to Trudeau. But the right hon. prime minister took his new seat in the front row of the west side of the House and rose immediately. "I had a speech," Pearson later told Tommy Douglas, the NDP leader and member for Burnaby-Coquitlam who walked across the floor to congratulate him. "I think it was a good one. I never got a chance to use it."

► **RIGHT HON. PIERRE TRUDEAU** — Prime Minister (Mount Royal): Mr. Speaker, I rise on a question of privilege. Speaking for the first time from this seat, I would ask the hon. members to allow me to express my thanks for the messages of congratulations I have received from all parts of the House. In a democracy, the people's representatives have a privilege to disagree on the best way of governing the country. However, we are all prompted by the same desire to make Canada a greater and a stronger country. The best answer I can give to that generous tribute is by undertaking to serve the House and the country to the best of my ability.

In view of the announcement I am about to make, Mr. Speaker, I feel that any further comment by me on any other subjects would be improper. This afternoon I called on the Governor General to request him to dissolve Parliament and to have writs issued for a general election on June 25. ◄

Technically, the House should not even have convened, for it stood dissolved from the moment the proclamation was signed. But it mattered little. Pierre Elliott Trudeau won the 1968 election and would remain prime minister of Canada for 11 uninterrupted years.

THE OPPOSITION IN HIS POCKET
►►►►►►►►►►►►►►►►►►►►►►

TRUDEAU HAD A LOVE-HATE relationship with Parliament. Having to deal with the consensus processes of cabinet and caucus seemed like such a hindrance to effective government decision-making. Throw in an opposition, and it was a clear waste of time. Yet the member for Mount Royal excelled in Parliament. No one, it seemed, could ruffle his feathers or catch him without an answer. During the first two years of the Twenty-eighth Parliament, his first as prime minister, his trademark was his quick delivery.

► *September 16, 1968*

RIGHT HON. PIERRE E. TRUDEAU — Prime Minister (Mount Royal): The leader of the opposition (Mr. Stanfield) claims that the speech from the throne rather surprised and disappointed him. He said it was a failure. The contrary would have surprised us.

In my opinion, had the speech been dictated by the Holy Spirit himself to the Governor General, the leader of the opposition would have deemed necessary to present a motion of non-confidence to the House.

February 7, 1969

STAN SCHUMACHER (Palliser): Mr. Speaker, my question is directed to the Right Hon. prime minister. In view of the universal affection with which the Queen Mother is held in this country, will not the government reconsider its decision to cancel the honour accorded her of a 21-gun salute on the occasion of her birthday?

MR. TRUDEAU: Mr. Speaker, we in this government believe that we should express our affection otherwise than by shooting guns.

January 14, 1970

PATRICK NOWLAN (Annapolis Valley): Mr. Speaker, my question is directed to the prime minister. It is succinct and in three parts, and I ask it that way for purposes of clarity and to avoid the necessity of supplementary questions. In light of the third report of the Bilingualism and Biculturalism Commission, has the government decided that it is necessary to review its policy with regards to bilingualism? If so, has it, and when will the prime minister make a statement?

MR. TRUDEAU: No, no, and never, Mr. Speaker.

March 19, 1970

HON. ROBERT STANFIELD — Leader of the Opposition (Halifax): With regard to the country as a whole, I should like to ask the prime minister whether it is the intention to pursue a policy of increasing unemployment?

MR. TRUDEAU: Is it the intention of the hon. member to stop beating his wife?

June 3, 1970

ROLAND GODIN (Portneuf): Mr. Speaker, I have a question for the prime minister. Could he tell the House whether, when he had a private meeting with the Ontario and Quebec premiers, Monday night, at the Queen Elizabeth hotel, the matter of the transfer of the family allowances plan to the provinces was brought up?

MR. TRUDEAU: Mr. Speaker, did the hon. member say that I attended a meeting? If he did, I must say I was not at such a meeting. Even if I had been, I would probably not tell the House, but, as I was not, I did not, of course, discuss that matter. ◀

10
A Period of Introspection
►►

THE OCTOBER CRISIS
►►►►►►►►►►►►►►►►

CHARLES DE GAULLE had come and gone, ignominiously ush-
ered out of the country after shouting an inflammatory
"Vive le Québec libre!" to a Montreal crowd. Political rhetoric
or genuine belief, it suddenly mattered little in October of 1970,
when a small group of made-in-Canada terrorists kidnapped the
British trade commissioner and the Quebec minister of labour
and immigration.

Since the battle of the Plains of Abraham, Canada had been
struggling with the accommodation of the first European immigrants, the francophones of Quebec. As confederation
spawned and European immigrants rushed to first fill the fertile
expanses of Upper Canada, and then the vast plains of the
prairie provinces, French-Canadians found their numerical
position in their North American partnership dwindling. As
early as 1867, anti-French sentiment was identifiable in English
Canada. To an outside observer, the independence of Quebec
may have seemed simply a matter of time.

By the latter half of the twentieth century, as a 1981 referendum would show, close to a majority of Quebecers were in
favour of independence. So perhaps, in the normal chronology
of nationalism, the violent outbreak in 1970 may have just been
the first bubble to burst.

Throughout the 1960s, there had been sporadic bombings of

property apparently belonging to *les Anglais*; many of the bombed buildings had freshly painted "FLQ" graffiti, the acronym of the Front de libération du Québec. And then, with whirlwind speed, the *crise d'octobre* exploded. Richard Cross, the British trade commissioner in Montreal, was abducted on October 5, 1970. The FLQ kidnappers issued ultimatums to the government of Quebec. As demanded, their long manifesto was read on Radio-Canada. Hoping to appease the kidnappers, Jérôme Choquette, the Quebec minister of justice, offered the abductors safe exit out of Canada to Cuba if they released Cross. In response, the provincial minister of labour and immigration, Pierre Laporte, was abducted on October 10.

In Ottawa, the prime minister watched in disbelief as the reports came in on the developments in his native province. He knew little of the size of the terrorist group but feared a concerted movement. On Wednesday, October 14, opposition leader Robert Stanfield, anticipating government action, asked that the government not invoke any emergency legislation without receiving parliamentary approval.

➤ **RIGHT HON. PIERRE TRUDEAU** — Prime Minister (Mount Royal): This is completely hypothetical. If such action were ever contemplated, it would certainly be discussed in the House. Whether it would be before or after would depend. It is obvious that if urgent action is needed at some time in the middle of the night, we cannot ask Parliament to approve it first.

GORDON AITKEN (Parry Sound-Muskoka): All these things happen in the middle of the night. ◀

Opposition premonitions were dead on. Both Montreal and Quebec authorities appeared disoriented in the crisis. Public hysteria was growing, and both local levels of government believed that insurrection might soon occur.

History would prove them wrong, as it was later discovered that the FLQ was but a tiny group of violent criminals. "Who are these men who are held out as latter-day patriots?" Trudeau asked during a later broadcast to Canadians. "Three are convicted murderers. Five others were jailed for manslaughter. Another has been convicted of 17 armed robberies."

But even Trudeau's police experts were unable to offer any substantial information on the magnitude of the threat. His minister of regional and economic expansion guessed that there might be as many as 3,000 armed FLQ terrorists. If he was to err, Trudeau decided to err on the side of caution. At emergency early morning cabinet meetings, it was decided to deploy troops in Montreal and Quebec City.

By the time Speaker Lucien Lamoureux called the members to order at 11 a.m. on Friday, October 16, 1970, news of the military police action was already dominating radio and television stations from coast to coast. The prime minister, having benefited from little sleep, rose and solemnly faced the House.

Trudeau took a few brief minutes of House time to confirm that the War Measures Act had been invoked by cabinet at four that morning. The act allowed the police to arrest and detain suspects for up to 90 days without the necessity of laying formal charges before a judge. Trudeau read a letter he had received at 3 a.m. from Premier Robert Bourassa of Quebec. "We are facing a concerted effort to intimidate and overthrow the government and the democratic institutions of this province through planned and systematic illegal action including insurrection," wrote Bourassa. "Not only are two completely innocent men threatened with death, but we are also faced with an attempt by a minority to destroy social order through criminal action." Trudeau then moved that the House give its unanimous consent to the cabinet decision.

When Trudeau sat down, Opposition Leader Robert Stanfield offered a partial endorsement of the government action, "for a limited period of time."

But the leader of the New Democratic Party, although he would face a hostile audience, offered a different opinion.

► **TOMMY DOUGLAS** (Nanaimo-Cowichan-The Islands): We have had civil disturbances in Canada before.

AN HON. MEMBER: Not like this one.

MR. DOUGLAS: Well, I recall as a boy the Winnipeg Strike.

MITCHELL SHARP — Secretary of State for External Affairs (Eglinton): But there was no kidnapping then.

FRANK HOWARD (Skeena): Why don't you listen, Mitch, and learn?

MR. DOUGLAS: This is the first time, to my knowledge, in Canadian history, that the War Measures Act has been invoked in peacetime. So far as the New Democratic Party is concerned, we have been prepared and are prepared to support enlarging the police powers. But, Mr. Speaker, we are not prepared to use the preservation of law and order as a smokescreen to destroy the liberties and the freedom of the people of Canada!

SOME HON. MEMBERS: Shame!

MR. DOUGLAS: I wonder if the Liberal members who are shouting "shame" have read the regulations?

PAUL LANGLOIS (Chicoutimi): The hon. member should go to Quebec and find out about the situation.

MR. DOUGLAS: The government, I submit, is using a sledgehammer to crack a peanut. This is overkill on a gargantuan scale! Today, the prime minister holds more power in his hands than any prime minister in the peacetime history of Canada!

AN HON. MEMBER: Thank God!

MR. DOUGLAS: The government now has the power by order in council to do anything it wants — to intern any citizen, to deport any citizen, to arrest any person or to declare any organization subversive or illegal. If the police in their judgement decide that some person is a member of a subversive organization — not just the FLQ but of any organization that the police decide is subversive or that he contributes to such a party . . .

AN HON. MEMBER: Why is the hon. member scared?

AN. HON. MEMBER: What has changed you, Tommy?

MR. DOUGLAS: . . . that person may be arrested and detained for 90 days, without any opportunity to prove his innocence. It is a resurrection of the padlock law.

NORMAN CAFIK (Ontario): Thank God the ship of state is not in your hands!

MR. DOUGLAS: I suggest, Mr. Speaker, that the action of the government constitutes a victory for the FLQ. They want a confrontation. They want the government and the people of Canada to consider that we are now engaged in a civil war with the FLQ.

The base of the FLQ lies in the disadvantaged and unfortunate people in the province of Quebec.

SOME HON. MEMBERS: Shame!

MR. DOUGLAS: No revolutionary movement can become a menace unless it has the support of the disadvantaged and alienated groups; the unemployed, the people who live in slums.

MR. TRUDEAU: This does not excuse violence.

MR. DOUGLAS: It does not. But the best way to stop people turning to violence is to remove the root causes which make them frustrated with the democratic process.

MR. TRUDEAU: And let Quebec separate? That is what they want.

MR. DOUGLAS: Police action alone will not prevent discontent and will not remove the sense of grievance and injustice which is felt by people. The FLQ will not go away until we deal with the discontent and the frustration in the hearts of five or six million Canadians who feel that this country is not giving them a fair chance. ◄

Such words were oddly reminiscent of James Woodsworth's 1939 speech in which he denounced the declaration of war against Germany, and Douglas too would pay a heavy political price for his opinion. Two months later, a Canadian Institute of Public Opinion poll asked whether respondents' opinion of Douglas had gone up or down as a result of his actions in the FLQ crisis: 36 per cent said it had gone down; only 8 per cent said it had gone up. Sixty per cent stated that their opinion of Trudeau had gone up during the crisis. More significantly, Gallup reported that the NDP crashed to 13 per cent in public support; down from 20 per cent in October. Four members of his New Democratic caucus broke ranks and voted in favour of Trudeau's resolution, which passed the House on October 19 with a whopping 190–16 majority. But by then, the crisis had intensified.

At 6:18 p.m., on Friday, October 16, while the debate on the resolution raged in the Commons, Pierre Laporte was executed by an FLQ cell. A Montreal radio station was sent an FLQ communiqué, and at midnight a military bomb squad pried open the trunk of an abandoned green Chevrolet outside the

St-Hubert military base. The trunk contained the bloody body of the provincial minister.

Premier Bourassa, unaware of the discovery, was in the midst of a public statement offering Cuban asylum to the FLQ members, provided that Cross and Laporte were freed. Word raced back to Ottawa and into the House of Commons just as Liberal Robert Borrie (Prince George-Peace River) was speaking. "This news has entrenched my opinion that the government has acted in a proper way," he commented. "We are not dealing with political dissenters. We are dealing with organized murderers." Out of respect for Laporte's family, the House quickly adjourned.

On November 6, police stormed the hideout of Laporte's murderers. They nabbed only one. Three others, Paul and Jacques Rose and Francis Simard, hid behind a false wall in a closet and escaped 24 hours later. On December 3, police cordoned off an apartment at 10945 des Récollets in Montreal and shut down the electrical supply. Inside were FLQ members Marc Carbonneau, Jacques Lanctôt and Yves Langlois and their hostage, Richard Cross. The standoff continued through the night. Finally, the abductors accepted the offer of asylum in Cuba. At noon the next day, the heavily armed terrorists and Cross entered an old Chrysler and drove to the Canadian pavilion on St. Helen's Island. Hours later they were in Cuba and Cross was free. On December 28, the Rose brothers and Simard were apprehended at a farmhouse near St.-Luc. The October Crisis was over.

FUDDLE-DUDDLE
►►►►►►►►►►

IT WAS QUESTION PERIOD, February 16, 1971. Prime Minister Trudeau was by now a six-year veteran of the House of Commons, but he continued to show little patience for an aggressive Conservative and New Democrat opposition, particularly in a time of rampant inflation and unemployment. The consumer price index for the month of February alone would reach 2.0, which meant an annual inflation rate of 24 per cent; unheard of in Canada.

A member took his cue from the Speaker and began to question the prime minister. Minutes later, members of the press gallery observed Trudeau mouthing the words "fuck you" towards opposition members. But as the expletive was never in fact spoken, it escaped the pages of Hansard. Evidently, however, it did not go unnoticed by the members on the opposition benches — or the media.

► **JOHN LUNDRIGAN** (Gander-Twillingate): Can I meekly, mildly and gently approach the esteemed and hon. gentleman who is occupying the throne of Canada at the moment. On behalf of 686,000 Canadians and myself, I would ask the hon. gentleman if he would condescend to tell us whether any new programs are to be announced now.... Let them eat what?!

JAMES MCGRATH (St. John's East): Shame on you! Say it for Hansard!

MR. SPEAKER — Lucien Lamoureux (Stormont-Dundas): Order! The hon. member for Gander-Twillingate seeks the floor on a point of order.

MR. LUNDRIGAN: On a question of privilege. I hope that the remark of the prime minister has been recorded. He does not have the guts to say to the people of Canada what he has just said across the floor of the House.

MR. SPEAKER: Order, please! Would the hon. member kindly resume his seat. He should state what his question of privilege is.

MR. LUNDRIGAN: Mr. Speaker, I am not permitted to use four-letter words in the House so I cannot quote for the record what the prime minister said. As a member of Parliament, I have all rights and privileges in representing my people and the people of the Canadian nation, including the right to present to the government any position or recommendation I think appropriate to alleviate unemployment. This attitude on the part of the prime minister is so contemptuous that it is certainly creating a tremendous amount of concern across Canada.

RIGHT HON. PIERRE E. TRUDEAU — Prime Minister (Mount Royal): Mr. Speaker, the hon. member has accused me of uttering a four-letter word in this House. That is an absolute untruth.

LINCOLN ALEXANDER (Hamilton West): Mr. Speaker, I want the record to show that after I referred the remark made by the prime minister back to him in terms indicating he had used this four-letter word twice, he then looked at me and used the same word again. Under no conditions do I have to sit here representing 100,000 people and accept the type of abuse that has been thrown not only at me but at every member of the opposition.

MR. TRUDEAU: Mr. Speaker, I challenge any member opposite to say that they heard me utter a single sound, and I challenge the Hansard reporter to say whether or not he has recorded anything of that sort. ◄

The press was waiting for the prime minister after Question Period. All he had done, replied Trudeau, was mouth "fuddle-duddle."

FAREWELL TO THE CHIEF
► ► ► ► ► ► ► ► ► ► ► ► ► ►

MONDAY, MARCH 26, 1979, was a special day in the history of the House of Commons. As it turned out, at nine in the evening the deputy prime minister and president of the Privy Council, Allan MacEachen (Cape Breton Highlands–Canso) announced that "the prime minister called on the Governor General a few moments ago. By proclamation under the great seal of Canada, dated March 26, 1979, the present Parliament of Canada is dissolved and members and senators are discharged from attendance. The date of the election is May 22."

Earlier in the day, however, another right hon. gentleman's voice had echoed through the hall of the Commons. The

83-year-old member for Prince Albert rose during Routine Proceedings to pay tribute to a recent and extraordinary international event.

► **RIGHT HON. JOHN DIEFENBAKER** (Prince Albert): Mr. Speaker, I rise under Standing Order 43 on an important matter on this historic date for all mankind. I move that this House express its deep appreciation to President Carter, to the Prime Minister of Israel and to the President of Egypt at having been successful at producing a treaty and, as the heads of these two countries have received the Nobel Peace Prize, and as each of them has spoken warmly of President Carter's contribution, that an award of the Nobel Peace Prize to him would be welcomed not only by Canadians but by peace-loving people of all mankind. ◄

Prime Minister Trudeau rose immediately, followed by New Democratic leader Ed Broadbent, both offering unanimous support to Diefenbaker's resolution. Referring to the former prime minister, Speaker James Jerome remarked that "there could scarcely be a more fitting way to celebrate the 39th anniversary of the Right Hon. gentleman's election to Parliament." They would also turn out to be the last words ever spoken in the House of Commons by John George Diefenbaker.

Two months later, Diefenbaker was re-elected in Prince Albert — marking the thirteenth time he had been elected to the House of Commons — as the Conservatives, under the leadership of Joe Clark, won the election. Only Sir Wilfrid Laurier had served in Parliament longer than Diefenbaker. But then, on August 16, 1979, in Ottawa, he passed away. A state funeral ensued, according to precise plans laid out by Diefenbaker himself, including a funeral train, which conveyed the body slowly across Canada to its final resting place beside the Diefenbaker Centre at the University of Saskatchewan.

On October 9, 1979, with Progressive Conservative Prime Minister Joe Clark sitting to the right of the Speaker, members rose to pay tribute. But the finest eulogy came from Pierre Trudeau, who, for the first time of his parliamentary career, found himself in the seat of leader of the opposition.

was one untoward incident, only one. The Liberal candidate in Central Nova persistently referred to a candidate from Quebec who did not live in his riding but lived in a million-dollar house rent free, and I defended you, Sir, regularly!

I was also delighted to read in the weekend press, Madam Speaker, the fact that the prime minister announced he is no quitter. I want you to know, Sir, that we are behind you all the way.

I want to say a few words of thanks as well to the hon. member for Oshawa (Mr. Broadbent). I want you to know that we Nova Scotians appreciate your judgement, Sir, in taking your caucus down to Nova Scotia. It did my heart good to see the socialists spending $90 and $95 a day, and then, prime minister, they have the temerity to say things are not going well!

SHANNON TWEED
►►►►►►►►►►►

JOHN CROSBIE'S UNSUCCESSFUL BID for the leadership of the Progressive Conservative party had cost more than $1 million. When the dust settled, Crosbie found himself short $200,000. But he still had the mukluks he wore the night before he handed down his ill-fated budget while minister of finance in Joe Clark's short-lived government. Crosbie's organizers decided to hold a fundraiser to look after Crosbie's deficit, and auction off the mukluks. They hired Helen Reddy and André Gagnon for music and thought an appearance by Playmate of the Year, Newfoundland-born Shannon Tweed, would sell a few tickets. On October 5, 1983, it was too much for one New Democratic member to pass up.

► **LORNE NYSTROM** (Yorkton-Melville): Madam Speaker, the member for St. John's West (Mr. Crosbie), the Conservative Finance critic, is reported to have a $200,000 deficit from his leadership campaign. Following in the footsteps of that world renowned feminist Hugh Hefner, the member is planning to pay off his debts by holding a little fund-raising bash to feature a former "Playboy" Playmate of the Year.

We all know of the Conservative party's impressive track record on women's issues as exemplified in its caucus where women make up only 3 per cent of its members. I am glad to see that traditional

Conservative sensitivity toward women is being upheld by the hon. member for St. John's West.

In fact, when questioned by the press as to the role of the playmate he said that she will not be the main course. He also said that he had abandoned the imaginative idea of wrapping his playmate in a Newfoundland flag and auctioning it off. He said, "someone would say it was sexist." He added, "you've got to be careful these days not to be sexist." And finally, he said, "there'll be nothing sexist going on there, at least not in public." ◀

Crosbie was not in the House when Nystrom criticized his fundraiser. However, he was at his roaring best when, a week later, he rose to respond.

▶ **JOHN CROSBIE** (St. John's West): Madam Speaker, a week ago the hon. member for Yorkton-Melville (Mr. Nystrom) attacked me in the House in my absence, about a concert which is to be held in Toronto at the Roy Thomson Hall. By the way, Madam Speaker, the concert is at 8 p.m. and is a fundraiser.

The hon. member claimed that I was being sexist because one of four performers at the concert is to be Miss Shannon Tweed, former Playboy Playmate of the Year.

Miss Tweed was born in Dildo, Trinity Bay, Madam Speaker, not far from Come-by-Chance. She is the daughter of a mainland mink farmer. Her talents will be used on the evening in question to auction the mukluks I wore when I brought down the budget on December 11, 1979. I ask the hon. member if the art of auctioning is sexist? Why does the hon. member attack my auctioneer? Having wrecked my budget together with the Liberal members opposite, he now seeks to wreck my auctioneer. The hon. member for Yorkton-Melville is certainly a bilious blue stocking, Madam Speaker. He is a yappy yokel and a slippery, sly sexual stereotyper, because that is what he has done. His actions are those of a sleeven.

Together, Miss Tweed and I will give the boot to the nasty Nystrom! ◀

Crosbie's debt was all but erased in that one night, as 2,800 tickets were sold at an average price of $75.

WOULD HE TABLE IT?
▶▶▶▶▶▶▶▶▶▶▶▶

THE **NEW DEMOCRATIC PARTY** has never formed a federal government, even though it has been trying since the 1935 election (as the Cooperative Commonwealth Federation).

Despite that, they have never lacked entertaining members. The trio of Ian Waddell, John Rodriguez (Nickel Belt) and Lorne Nystrom (Yorkton-Melville) have often kept the floor rocking well into the wee hours of the morning, on many an emergency debate. And so it was on January 25, 1985, on a cold, snowy Friday morning in Ottawa that Waddell rose, poised to address the Speaker. If the dress code was ever to be tested, this would be the day.

▶ **IAN WADDELL** (Vancouver-Kingsway): I rise on a point of order, Mr. Speaker. Today is, of course, Robbie Burns Day which, traditionally, Scottish Canadians celebrate. I am wearing my kilt. I am a little unclear about the dress code in the House. I seek your permission, Sir, to be able to sit in the House while wearing a kilt. Considering that this country really was started by French-Canadians and Scots, I think I should be allowed to do so.

SHEILA FINESTONE (Mont-Royal): On the point of order, Mr. Speaker, I will say that I have no objection as long as the hon. member is prepared to share with us the knowledge of what he is wearing under that kilt.

MR. WADDELL: Mr. Speaker, may I reply to my hon. friend who, I might say, I respect and admire. She is a very articulate new member of the House of Commons, and I do not say that in a Burnsian sense. I can only say to the hon. member that nothing is worn under the kilt. It is all in perfect working order.

LORNE NYSTROM (Yorkton-Melville): Mr. Speaker, I just wonder if the hon. member for Vancouver-Kingsway would table it?

GORDON TAYLOR (Bow River): On a point of order, Mr. Speaker, a dead bird cannot fall from its nest!

DOUGLAS FRITH (Sudbury): I rise on the same point of order, Mr. Speaker. I just want the House to know that the Liberal party does not want to nationalize it either!

ACTING SPEAKER — JEAN CHAREST (Sherbrooke): Before resuming debate, I will inform the member for Vancouver-Kingsway that this House today, I believe, will accept his dress code as long as he does not, of course, make a habit of it.

DENNIS COCHRANE (Moncton): Mr. Speaker, I am almost afraid to speak in case I lower the high level of this debate!

THE MEECH LAKE ACCORD AND BEYOND
►►►►►►►►►►►►►►►►►►►►►►►►►►►►►►

F**EW POLITICAL EVENTS** have ever caused more structural consternation in the Dominion of Canada than did the 1987 Meech Lake accord, the constitutional agreement reached by 10 premiers and Prime Minister Brian Mulroney at a federal government retreat at Meech Lake, near Ottawa, on April 30. In spite of the wave of satisfaction that went through the nation's capital when the accord was signed 34 days later, the agreement would soon writhe pitifully upon the political landscape of Canada, condemned to fall prey to dissidence amongst the 11 legislative assemblies that had to approve it within three years. In its wake, the country would be thrust into constitutional incertitude the likes of which had not been seen since Confederation.

Quebec had refused to sign a 1982 amendment to the Constitution, the project of prime minister and Liberal leader Pierre Trudeau. Although, legally, it still applied to all of Canada, only the government of Quebec had yet to officially accept the changes. It was a political dilemma, and one that did little to lessen the separatist sentiments that some Quebecers still harboured towards Canada.

At first, the Meech Lake accord appeared to have unstoppable political momentum. In addition to the consent of all 10 provincial premiers, the accord benefited from the immediate support of national Liberal leader John Turner and of the leader of the New Democratic Party, Ed Broadbent. Both were painfully aware of the political necessity of accommodating the long-outstanding constitutional demands of a succession of Quebec governments.

When the premiers met with Mulroney in Ottawa, on June 2, to put the final touches on the legal text of their April 30 agreement, last-minute hitches caused the group to stay convened for 19½ hours. Finally, at 5:30 the next morning, the deal was signed. That afternoon, the prime minister walked into the chamber amidst thunderous applause from all corners of the House. He walked over and shook Turner's and Broadbent's hands. When the applause subsided, Speaker John Fraser gave the leader of the opposition the floor. "When the Prime Minister of Canada comes over to shake my hand," Turner began, "I shake his hand. But before congratulating him, we will want to study the technical and legal language."

Thus began the tumultuous journey of the accord through the legislatures of the nation. On June 23, the government of Quebec ratified the accord and set in motion the three-year clock within which all ten provincial legislative assemblies and Parliament had to ratify the Meech Lake resolutions. Two months later, Saskatchewan became the second province to ratify the accord.

And then, the first cracks in the lacquer began to appear. Interest groups and constitutional experts began to question perceived shortcomings of the accord. On August 27, former prime minister Pierre Trudeau appeared before a House of Commons committee tasked with studying the accord and asked the question that was on everybody's mind. "Assuming distinct society means something," the 67-year-old Trudeau said, "why does Quebec need a special status?" This and other concessions to the provinces, such as the right to nominate Senate and Supreme Court candidates or the right to opt out of national federal social programs, were anathema to the many Canadians who feared losing a dominant central government.

The committee failed to produce a unanimous report. On October 6, Mulroney could only watch in sullen disappointment as one of his own backbenchers rose to speak in the House against the accord.

"Meech Lake will be remembered in the North as one of the most shameful events in Canadian history," said David Nickerson, the member for Western Arctic. "An event where representatives of southern Canada got together as a cozy little club and decided to blackball the people of the North. We have lost the Meech Lake battle! But we have not lost the war! Not by a long shot!"

Less than a week after Nickerson had spoken, one of the 11 signatories of the accord was thrown out of office as the New Brunswick Liberal party swept every seat in the provincial election. Premier-elect Frank McKenna refused to endorse his predecessor's signature on the accord. But then, as if in natural retort to the new threat, the House moved to the final moments of debate on the accord on October 21, 1987.

The outcome of the vote in the House of Commons, 242–16 in favour of the accord, seemed to give the deal new momentum. The government of Alberta endorsed the accord on December 7, 1987. Howard Pawley, another of the accord's signatories, was defeated in a Manitoba election held on April 26 and was replaced by a Progressive Conservative premier, Gary Filmon.

Prince Edward Island ratified the agreement on May 13, 1988, and Nova Scotia, on May 25. A legal appeal by the government of the Yukon against the proposed accord was rejected by the Supreme Court. When the accord was returned to the Commons from the Senate on June 14, 1988, the prime minister delivered the speech the country had been waiting for.

► **RIGHT HON. BRIAN MULRONEY** — Prime Minister (Manicouagan): Mr. Speaker, it is time, once and for all, for the rest of Canada to say yes to Quebec. And the way to do so is to proceed with ratification of the Meech Lake Accord.

Our country's constitutional development did not end with the British North America Act of 1867. It did not end with the Statute of Westminster in 1931. It did not end with the Constitution Act of 1982. And it will not end with the Meech Lake Accord of 1987. At every stage of our constitutional history, as we have settled the agenda of one generation, we have gained the freedom to move on to the next.

And so it was, Mr. Speaker, after the BNA of 1867 which settled the powers of the federal government and the provinces and established the goal of "peace, order and good government" in the management of our national affairs; and so it was after the Statute of Westminster of 1931 which saw our nation achieve autonomy in the conduct of foreign affairs; and so it was after the Constitution Act of 1982 which saw patriation of our Constitution and the entrenchment of the Charter; and in the next round which will take place, Mr. Speaker, just as surely as summer follows spring in Canada, we will deal with the outstanding issues of Senate reform, aboriginal rights, and enhancing the role of linguistic and cultural minorities in Canada.

Are we as a Parliament, as a people, to hold Quebec's constitutional reintegration hostage to the pursuit of perfection in these other areas? Let us not make the perfect the enemy of the good. Surely, we have a much better chance to improve our Constitution with Quebec as a full participant at the table. Surely, no government in its right senses would try to proceed to these other issues without the participation of Quebec.

Mr. Speaker, this is not a unitary state. Regardless of what some people claim, Ottawa is not the omnipresent, omnipotent source of wisdom and power in this land. There are those who say that too much has been given to obtain Quebec's signature. And there are those in Quebec who say that we have not conceded enough. On the one hand, you have those who regard themselves as being in sole possession of the truth, who have always treated Quebec's legitimate aspirations with ill-concealed contempt. On the other hand, you have those who have always rebuffed sincere efforts at reconciling Quebec's legitimate needs with the national interest, whose only interest in constitutional discussions is to sever links with the rest of Canada. And somewhere in between, Mr. Speaker, you have the vast majority of people who regard Quebec as their home, but Canada as their country.

We have affirmed the linguistic duality of our nation, and the distinctiveness Quebec brings to our country. This constitutional arrangement simply reflects reality. Not that Quebec is special, just that it is different and distinct within Canada. Language and culture in particular give rise to this fact.

We do not close our eyes to Quebec's distinctiveness within Canada. Rather, we embrace it, for it enriches our national culture and strengthens our national identity as Canadians on the northern half of this continent.

I am proud of the Meech Lake Accord. Canada is one of the world's youngest nations but one of the world's oldest democracies. It is a country with an Atlantic heritage and a Pacific perspective. It truly is a land for tomorrow, perhaps the most bountiful and blessed country on the face of the earth. In this beloved country, enriched by wave after wave of immigrants coming from around the world to build a tolerant and splendid new society on the northern half of this continent, the Accord brings us together as a people. That is our point of departure with Meech Lake, building one Canada, united and strong. ◄

For a second time, the House of Commons endorsed the accord. A week later, the Ontario and British Columbia legislative assemblies followed suit. On July 7, the Progressive Conservative government in Newfoundland secured a ratification vote from the assembly in Saint John. This left only New Brunswick and Manitoba, and a full 23 months before the June 23, 1990, deadline. In November 1988, Mulroney's Progressive Conservative government was re-elected.

The beginning of the end of the Meech Lake accord came just before Christmas 1988. Responding to restrictive language legislation passed by the Quebec national assembly, Gary Filmon retaliated by withdrawing the Meech Lake accord resolution from the order paper of the Manitoba legislative assembly. Then, Clyde Wells, an avowed opponent of the accord, led his Liberal party to victory in a Newfoundland election on April 20.

John Turner announced his resignation from the leadership of the federal Liberal party on May 3, crippling his ability to exert influence on his caucus members. The leading candidate was Jean Chrétien, who had declared his opposition to the accord. Edward Broadbent also resigned in the spring of 1989, and was replaced by Audrey McLaughlin. Earlier, McLaughlin had broken ranks with Broadbent and voted against the accord in the House of Commons.

Clyde Wells led the Newfoundland assembly on April 6 in rescinding its earlier ratification, prompting Quebec's intergovernmental affairs minister, Gil Remillard, to remark that "Canada can survive very well without Newfoundland." Desperation, a poor substitute for cooperation, had set in. The death of the Meech Lake accord was not long to follow.

The premiers and the prime minister reconvened in Ottawa

on June 3 in a last-minute attempt to save the accord. Six days later, they parted with an apparent agreement to pass the accord before the June 23 deadline, now only two weeks away.

New Brunswick approved the accord on June 15. But the clock struck midnight on Saturday, June 22, with the Meech Lake accord still short two provincial endorsements.

In the aftermath of the failure of the Meech Lake accord, federal and provincial politicians returned to the dreaded predicament of constitutional impasse. Quebec immediately announced it would no longer attend federal-provincial meetings.

Slowly and tentatively, national catharsis began. Numerous federal and provincial constitutional consultations and studies were undertaken. Conferences were called. Aboriginal people and their concerns were included in the discussions. Issues such as Senate reform were discussed, the clauses of the defunct Meech Lake accord serving as ideals from which more comprehensive agreements could be reached and bringing more and more Canadians into the fold of national constitutional consensus.

Canada has been to the brink before. Each time, the people have pulled it back. For example, in 1865-66, the Confederation proposals were actually defeated in elections or in the legislative assemblies of New Brunswick, Newfoundland and Prince Edward Island. In the Quebec national assembly, Confederation was approved by a far from unanimous 37–25 vote. The Nova Scotia assembly approved a union of British North America by a 31–19 vote. Since 1867, both Nova Scotia (1886) and Quebec (1976) have elected separatist governments. Both failed in their ultimate objective. Canada and its provinces will continue to challenge and improve upon the constitutional structure upon which it is based. The process will never completely end. That is the price of cutting-edge democracy.

Epilogue
▶▶▶▶▶▶▶▶▶▶▶

SINCE THAT COLD November day in 1867 when Lord Monck presided over the opening of the First Session of the First Parliament of the government of the new Dominion of Canada, the House of Commons has served as the boardroom of the affairs of the nation. Events such as the Riel rebellions, two world wars, ministerial resignations, economic depression, social programs and political scandals have marked the pages of the debates of the House. It is where the most famous of Canadians, such as John A. Macdonald, George-Etienne Cartier, Wilfrid Laurier, Mackenzie King, James Woodsworth and Pierre Trudeau, have left their intellectual legacy. There have been moments of chaos; moments where firecrackers have been thrown across the floor of the House; moments where physical skirmishes have broken out; moments where careers have been lost or launched.

In recent times, the House of Commons has been criticized. The roles of the opposition and non-cabinet members have oft been dubbed as inconsequential. Where government appears to be the purview of a few elite politicians, the prime minister first amongst them, many wonder why spend tens of millions of dollars on a national debating society? The public perception of the House's utility is further exacerbated by the regulatory demands of a modern-day state — many of the important decisions of government are taken by departments or Crown corporations.

This public opinion is the standard of consecutive majority governments. A prime minister and cabinet gain the confidence of the public service, gather momentum until their legislative program seems to cruise through the House. Macdonald, Laurier, King, St. Laurent, Trudeau and Brian Mulroney have all enjoyed such extended terms.

But the checks and balances of a British-inspired Canadian House of Commons remain intact, ready to respond and provide peaceful resolution to questions of state. "We enjoy the privileges of constitutional liberty according to the British system," said Sir John A. Macdonald, arguing the case for Confederation before the assembly of the Province of Canada in 1865. "It is only in countries like England, enjoying constitutional liberty, and safe from the tyranny of a single despot or of an unbridled democracy, that the rights of the minorities are regarded."

For example, if a federal election does not provide a clear incumbent to the prime ministership, it remains the Governor General's prerogative to select a first minister. Moreover, at any time, a motion of non-confidence may be placed against a government in the House, the success of which would cause its immediate resignation. Political caucuses or not, proposed laws must always be put to vote three times in the House. The Canadian House of Commons remains eternally vigilant, above the absolute control of any individual, in the best of times as well as in the worst of dangers.

It is the most important of Canada's national institutions, one worth the respect, study and attention of every citizen, *a mari usque ad mare*.

SELECTED
BIBLIOGRAPHY
▶▶▶▶▶▶▶▶▶▶▶▶▶▶▶▶▶▶▶▶▶

Abbott, Elizabeth, ed., *Chronicle of Canada*. Montreal: Chronicle Publications, 1990.

Anderson, Frank W., *The Riel Rebellion 1885*. Calgary: Frontier Publishing, 1968.

Beck, J. Murray, ed., *Joseph Howe: The Voice of Nova Scotia*. Toronto: McClelland and Stewart, 1964.

Biggar, Emerson Bristol, *An Anecdotal Life of Sir John A. Macdonald*. Montreal: John Lovell & Son, 1891.

Borden, Robert L., *Robert Laird Borden: His Memoirs* (2 vols.). Toronto: Macmillan of Canada, 1938.

Bosc, Marc, ed., *The Broadview Book of Canadian Parliamentary Anecdotes*. Peterborough: Broadview Press, 1988.

Bothwell, Robert et. al., *Canada 1900–1945*. Toronto: University of Toronto Press, 1987.

Buckingham, William and Geo. W. Ross, *The Hon. Alexander Mackenzie: His Life and Times*. Toronto: Rose Publishing, 1892.

Butson, Thomas, *Pierre Elliott Trudeau*. New York: Chelsea House, 1986.

Canada, Parliament. *House of Commons Debates,* 1867–1992.

Canada, Public Archives of Canada. *The Canadian Directory of Parliament.* Ottawa: Queen's Printer, 1968.

Canadian Parliamentary Companion, 1868–1897.

Careless, J.M.S., *Brown of the Globe* (2 vols.). Toronto: Macmillan of Canada, 1963.

Cartwright, Sir Richard, *Reminiscences.* Toronto: William Briggs, 1912.

Charlesworth, Hector, *Candid Chronicles.* Toronto: Macmillan of Canada, 1925.

Clarkson, Stephen and Christina McCall, *Trudeau and Our Times: The Magnificent Obsession.* Toronto: McClelland and Stewart, 1991.

Colombo, John Robert, ed., *Colombo's Canadian Quotations.* Edmonton: Hurtig Publishers, 1974.

Creighton, Donald, *John A. Macdonald: The Old Chieftain.* Toronto: Macmillan of Canada, 1955.

Creighton, Donald, *John A. Macdonald: The Young Politician.* Toronto: Macmillan of Canada, 1956.

Creighton, Donald, *The Road to Confederation.* Toronto: Macmillan of Canada, 1964.

Diefenbaker, John G., *One Canada: The Memoirs of the Right Hon. John G. Diefenbaker.* Toronto: Macmillan of Canada, 1975.

Donaldson, Gordon, *Eighteen Men.* Toronto: Doubleday Canada, 1985.

Fleming, Donald, *So Very Near: The Political Memoirs of the Hon. Donald M. Fleming* (2 vols.). Toronto: McClelland and Stewart, 1985.

Gordon, Walter L., *A Political Memoir*. Toronto: McClelland and Stewart, 1977.

Graham, Roger, *Arthur Meighen* (3 vols.). Toronto: Clarke, Irwin & Company, 1960, 1963, 1965.

Gwyn, Richard J., *The Shape of Scandal*. Toronto: Clarke, Irwin & Company, 1965.

Gwyn, Richard, *The Northern Magus*. Toronto: McClelland and Stewart, 1980.

Gwyn, Sandra, *The Private Capital*. Toronto: McClelland and Stewart Limited, 1984.

Hardy, H. Reginald, *Mackenzie King of Canada*. Toronto: Oxford University Press, 1949.

Hopkins, J. Castell, *Life and Work of the Rt. Hon. Sir John Thompson*. Brantford: Bradley, Garreston & Co., 1895.

Howard, Joseph Kinsey, *Strange Empire*. New York: William Morrow and Company, 1952.

Hutchison, Bruce, *Mr. Prime Minister*. Don Mills: Longmans Canada, 1964.

Hutchison, Bruce, *The Incredible Canadian*. Toronto: Longmans, Green and Co., 1952.

Locke, George, *Builders of the Canadian Commonwealth*. Toronto: The Ryerson Press, 1923.

Longley, J.W., *Sir Charles Tupper*. Toronto: Makers of Canada (Morang), 1916.

MacInnis, Grace, *J.S. Woodsworth: A Man to Remember*. Toronto: Macmillan of Canada, 1953.

Maclean, Andrew D., *R.B. Bennett*. Toronto: Excelsior Publishing Company, 1935.

MacLeod, Jack, ed., *The Oxford Book of Canadian Political Anecdotes*. Toronto: Oxford University Press, 1988.

Macpherson, J. Pennington, *Life of the Right Hon. Sir John A. Macdonald* (2 vols.). St. John: Earle Publishing House, 1891.

Marsh, James H., ed., *The Canadian Encyclopedia* (4 vols.). Edmonton: Hurtig Publishers, 1988.

Martin, Paul, *A Very Public Life* (2 vols.). Toronto: Deneau Publishers, 1985.

McKenty, Neil, *Mitch Hepburn*. Toronto: McClelland and Stewart, 1967.

McLeod, Thomas H. and Ian McLeod, *Tommy Douglas: The Road to Jerusalem*. Edmonton: Hurtig Publishers, 1987.

Meighen, Arthur, *Unrevised and Unrepented*. Toronto: Clarke, Irwin & Company, 1949.

Morton, Desmond, *A Short History of Canada*. Edmonton: Hurtig Publishers, 1983.

Nash, Knowlton, *Kennedy and Diefenbaker*. Toronto: McClelland and Stewart, 1990.

Neary, Peter and O'Flaherty, Patrick, *Part of the Main: An Illustrated History of Newfoundland and Labrador*. St. John's: Breakwater Books, 1985.

Neatby, H. Blair, *William Lyon Mackenzie King: The Lonely Heights*. Toronto: University of Toronto Press, 1963.

Newman, Peter, *Renegade in Power*. Toronto: McClelland and Stewart, 1963.

Newman, Peter, *The Distemper of Our Times*. Toronto: McClelland and Stewart, 1968.

O'Leary, Grattan, *Recollections of People, Press, and Politics*. Toronto: Macmillan of Canada, 1977.

Parliamentary Guide, 1898–1992.

Pearson, Lester B., *Memoirs of Lester B. Pearson* (3 vols.). Toronto: University of Toronto Press, 1972, 1973, 1975.

Pearson, Lester B., *Words and Occasions*. Toronto: University of Toronto Press, 1970.

Pickersgill, J.W. and D.F. Foster, *The Mackenzie King Record* (4 vols.). Toronto: University of Toronto Press, 1960, 1970.

Pope, Joseph, *Memoirs of the Right Honourable Sir John A. Macdonald* (2 vols.). Ottawa: J. Durie & Son, 1894.

Pope, Joseph, *The Day of Sir John Macdonald*. Toronto: Glasgow, Brook & Company, 1915.

Preston, W.T.R., *The Life and Times of Lord Strathcona*. Toronto: McClelland, Goodchild & Stewart, 1941.

Saunders, E.M., *The Life and Letters of the Rt. Hon. Sir Charles Tupper, Bart., K.C.M.G.* Toronto: Cassell and Company, 1916.

Schull, Joseph, *Edward Blake: Leader and Exile*. Toronto: Macmillan of Canada, 1976.

Schull, Joseph, *Laurier: The First Canadian*. Toronto: Macmillan of Canada, 1965.

Shortt, Adam and Arthur G. Doughty, *Canada and Its Provinces* (23 vols.). Edinburgh: Edinburgh University Press (for the Publishers Association of Canada), 1914–17.

Skelton, Oscar Douglas, *Life and Times of Sir Alexander Tilloch Galt*. Toronto: Oxford University Press, 1920.

Skelton, Oscar Douglas, *Life and Letters of Sir Wilfrid Laurier* (2 vols.). Toronto: Oxford University Press, 1921.

Stursberg, Peter, *Lester Pearson and the Dream of Unity*. Toronto: Doubleday Canada, 1978.

Swettenham, John, *McNaughton* (3 vols.). Toronto: The Ryerson Press, 1968.

Thompson, Dale C., *Alexander Mackenzie, Clear Grit*. Toronto: Macmillan of Canada, 1960.

Thompson, Dale C., *Louis St. Laurent, Canadian*. Toronto: Macmillan of Canada, 1967.

Troyer, Warner, *200 Days: Joe Clark in Power.* Toronto: Personal Library Publishers, 1980.

Tupper, Sir Charles, *Recollections of Sixty Years in Canada.* Toronto: Cassell and Co., 1914.

Wallace, W. Stewart, *The Memoirs of the Rt. Hon. Sir George Foster.* Toronto: Macmillan of Canada, 1933.

Wilbur, Richard, *H. H. Stevens.* Toronto: University of Toronto Press, 1977.

Young, James, *Public Men and Public Life in Canada* (2 vols.). Toronto: William Briggs, 1912.

INDEX

▶▶▶▶▶▶▶▶

*Ridings indicated in **bold**.*